PSYCHOANALYTIC INQUIRY

A Topical Journal for Mental Health Professionals

Volume 11 | 1991 | Number 3

Recent Developments in the Concept and Treatment of Phobias and Panic States

Routledge
Taylor & Francis Group
New York London

Routledge is an imprint of the
Taylor & Francis Group, an informa business

PSYCHOANALYTIC INQUIRY

ISSN 0735-1690

Editorial Note

WE WANT TO ACKNOWLEDGE changes in our editorial group. After many valuable contributions, seven of our members have rotated off. We want to thank Raphael Gonzalez, issue co-editor of "Commentaries on Ping-Nie Pao's Schizophrenic Disorders"; Martin Mayman, issue editor of "Infant Research: The Dawn of Awareness"; Sydney Smith, issue editor of "Adolescent Addiction: Varieties and Vicissitudes"; John Mack, issue editor of "Aggression and Its Alternatives in the Conduct of International Relations"; and Richard Isay, Stanley Greenspan, and A. Scott Dowling, who served as co-editors and authors on a number of issues.

We welcome as new editors Martin Silverman, Owen Renik, Robert Stolorow, Donald Ross, Estelle Shane, and George Moraitis. We appreciate the contributions our new editors have already made and look forward eagerly to their continued creativity and assistance.

We also want to acknowledge the ongoing special gifts of our manuscript editor, Natalie Altman, whose title does not come close to designating her value to our success.

Joseph D. Lichtenberg, M.D.
Editor-in-Chief

Prologue

PHOBIAS AND PANIC STATES have in recent years become the subject of intense interest in psychiatry. Psychiatric journals are flooded with publications on the biological and behavioral aspects of these conditions which have to some extent obstructed the reader's awareness of the contributions of psychoanalysis to the understanding and treatment of these conditions. It would be ironic if, during this period of the widening scope of the clinical applications of psychoanalytic treatment, the psychoanalyst were to relinquish to the nonanalytically oriented therapist this crucial clinical field upon which psychoanalytic theory and its clinical applications are based.

By devoting this issue of *Psychoanalytic Inquiry* to the recent advances in the psychoanalytic understanding and treatment of phobias, we aim to provide our readers with a more balanced view of our present knowledge about phobias, and alert them to the fact that the contemporary psychoanalyst shares with Freud his intense interest in the subject and continues the search for a more effective conceptualization and treatment of these conditions, which takes into account new data and observations from within and without the field of psychoanalysis.

The classical approach in analyzing phobias aims to uncover the unconscious fantasy operating behind the symptom and reconstruct the original trauma, facilitating in the process the patient's capacity to come to terms with it. The original trauma may be an actual experience or a fantasy, and is conceptualized as the point of origin of the neurosis and the central focus of the psychoanalytic enterprise. The psychoanalytic literature of phobias has provided us with imaginative and creative reconstructions based on Freud's formulations about the fear of castration and the aggressive impulses associated with it. More contemporary psychoanalytic thinkers have, however, conceptualized certain fundamental structural deficits upon which the phobic symptomatology rests. Accordingly, these investigators are less likely to focus on the symbolic meaning of the patient's behavior and associations. Instead, they conceptualize the phobic symptom as only one manifestation of a more basic defect in the personality structure. This approach has important clinical implications.

Freud always maintained the distinction between phobias as a psychoneurotic symptom and phobias as an actual neurosis which lacks symbolic content, but he placed increasingly less emphasis on the actual neurosis as his thinking evolved. The recent developments in the conceptualization of phobias have rekindled interest in Freud's earlier formulations, especially because they resonate with the biological aspects of the symptom, for which new data are available from neurobiology.

We have invited our contributors to reexamine phobias in the light of their own convictions and personal experiences and to provide us with additional insights and, if possible, integration. Our contributors were selected because of their interest in the subject, their sense of historical background, and their capacity to approach it from a contemporary perspective. They were provided with maximum freedom to tailor their contribution to their own interests and concerns. With one exception. David Spira was asked to summarize the evolution of Freud's thinking on the subject of phobias in an effort to refresh the reader's awareness of the complexities involved and Freud's lifelong effort to come to terms with them.

W.W. Meissner sees phobia as inextricably tied to the expression of aggression, which he conceptualizes as a "drive capacity" requiring appropriate stimulation to elicit response. Meissner believes that "the dynamics of phobic formations reach beyond issues of mere drive and defense, that they impinge on more persistent characterological and structural levels of personality organization."

John Gedo addresses some of the issues of phobic avoidance that are "beyond interpretation," which Meissner alluded to. More specifically, Gedo describes the phobic patient's sense of shame and humiliation when confronted with anxiety and affect-laden situations, as well as his inability to make use of symbolization and displacement. Gedo defines these phenomena as apraxias indicative of the archaic origin of these symptoms, and the psychoanalytic treatment of these conditions as a "technology of remedial education in a series of missing skills."

George Moraitis conceptualizes phobias as the fear of the unknown, based on the patient's inability to assimilate and accomodate novel input. The search for novelty is conceptualized as a motivational force in its own right that operates in opposition to the need to reproduce and reenact the past. Moraitis, too, identifies two basic types of phobias, but he addresses primarily those for which the main therapeutic aim is to increase the patient's capacity to deal with ambiguity and unfamiliarity.

Another contribution is coauthored by Frederick Bush, Arnold Cooper, Gerald Klerman, Robert Renzer, Theodore Shapiro, and Katherine Shear. The authors first summarize the biological, behavioral, and psychological aspects of panic disorders in order to inform the reader of the extent and limitations of the knowledge each of those fields contributes to the understanding and treatment of panic disorders. They then offer an integrating schema for the understanding of these conditions that postulates a neurophysiological and psychological vulnerability to panic based on an inborn excessive fearfulness of unfamiliar situations that leads to heightened dependency on the parent. This fearful dependency becomes the "source of narcissistic humiliations for the child, . . . elicits feelings of helplessness and demonstrates to him his own incapacity for handling the unfamiliar."

Jon Meyer and Vladimir Maletic begin with a description of the evolution of the perspectives on phobias and proceed to identify with clinical examples two kinds of phobias, those which are part of a larger symptom complex and those which represent the core of the neurosis and can be compared to perversion. The authors emphasize the importance of the attachment to the phobic object, which accounts for its dangerousness.

Barbara Rocah offers a presentation and discussion of an unsuccessful analysis of a severely phobic patient as a basis for suggesting that the phobia was an example of traumatic neurosis that has triggered a systemic disease containing "an admixture of conflictual, post-traumatic dysfunctional, and dysregulatory elements, as well as characterological adaptations to these developmental vicissitudes."

As I mentioned earlier, David Spira's paper is offered to provide an opportunity to consider Freud's long struggle to master the complexities of phobias.

In closing the issue, Joseph Lichtenberg reviews its contributions and places phobias into the broad context of anxiety and its developmental vicissitudes. Lichtenberg deciphers important questions raised by our contributors, directly or indirectly, and offers his own integrating schema.

This issue has been prepared in the hope that it will offer its readers a good deal to reflect on that will be of assistance in their efforts to cope with the sense of strangeness and bewilderment that the phobic symptom and its tenacity arouses in the analyst. Furthermore, it is hoped that the material presented will contribute to a deeper appreciation of the ambiguity of the clinical situation and the need to avoid unwarranted presumptions of knowledge when dealing with phobias.

George Moraitis, M.D.
Issue Editor

Aggression in Phobic States

W. W. MEISSNER, S.J., M.D.

IN PREVIOUS PAPERS INTRODUCING ANOTHER PERSPECTIVE on the psychoanalytic theory of aggression (Buie et al., 1983; Meissner et al., 1987), our study group on aggression presented what we felt was a more authentically psychoanalytic and more purely motivational understanding of aggression that suited the findings on and the vicissitudes of it as manifested in the psychoanalytic process.

The essential elements of that understanding can be summarized as follows:

1. Aggression is not simply a biologically based drive in a constant state of activity or discharge, but a biologically rooted drive capacity that requires appropriate stimulus conditions to elicit activation or response.

This view of aggression clearly diverges from the classical drive notion. The difference is clear in the developmental context: drive theory would see the development of aggression as a process in which the mental apparatus strives to integrate the aggressive drive derivatives impinging on it from below, i.e., from an innate biologically given drive; our motivational theory would see the development in aggression as reflecting the organism's experience of dealing with and overcoming obstacles in the course of which drive potentialities or capacities are activated and integrated. Aggression is thus a given capacity that comes into play only under

Dr. Meissner is Training and Supervising Analyst, Boston Psychiatric Institute; and University Professor of Psychoanalysis, Boston College.

appropriate stimulus or motivational conditions. Aggression is thus less of a biological force, and becomes more a psychological construct related to and reactive to specifiable stimulus conditions, including relationships with objects. The emphasis shifts from the biological determinants to the motivational context of aggressive action. The biological substrate remains intact, but is no longer the important determining element.

2. The motivational (as opposed to drive-discharge) aspect of this model of aggression arises from the conditions of activation, namely, the need for activating stimuli, the goal-oriented or purposeful character of the response, and its inherent connection with wishes, desires, meanings, and intentions.

Motivation in a general sense refers to a disposition to purposive or intentional action, whether conscious or unconscious. Motivation in this sense is distinct from sheer energic discharge, although it may involve energic components. Motives may express themselves in varying degrees of complexity, intensity, modes of displacement, and levels of psychic integration (Klein, 1967). Wishes, in this hierarchy of motivational terms, are not merely expressions of drive impulse or discharge, but include a cognitive dimension, which lends direction and intention to the drive expression, usually through linkage with a mnemic image. In Freud's view, the fulfillment of a wish is a psychic act aimed at reproducing "the perceptions, which have become the signs of . . . satisfaction" (Laplanche & Pontalis, 1973, p. 482). Motivation intends the achievement of a particular aim. The aim may be the satisfaction of a need, the fulfillment of a wish, the attainment of psychic equilibrium, or the avoidance of distressful affect. Any interference with the accomplishment of the aim of a motivation becomes an obstacle. The obstacle may be extrinsic to the individual or intrapsychic.

Once a mental representation of a motivational aim has been formed, an action is elicited to obtain it. If an obstacle interferes, the ego may call any available psychic process into play to overcome it. Aggression utilizes any resource of the organism, from physical force to defense mechanisms, in its persistence toward reaching the motivational goal. Aggression thus requires the participation of several psychic agencies and a rearrangement of the defensive system. Certain aggressive behaviors involve a minimal number of psychic processes, while others may require the participation of all three psychic agencies. In this view aggression is not a force, but an action capacity for integrating psychic functions in the service of attaining a motivational aim.

3. The common element in aggressive behaviors is the striving or exertion for the purpose of overcoming an obstacle. In the clinical setting such obstacles are exclusively nonphysical insofar as they can be cast meaningfully in either psychological or moral terms. Aggression only comes into play when an action that is otherwise naturally, easily, or comfortably effected is inhibited, impeded, or otherwise counteracted by an obstacle. By implication, therefore, it is not the action that determines the aggressive nature of the activity, but rather its motivation, i.e., overcoming the obstacle. Consequently, even destructive actions would not be aggressive specifically because of their destructiveness, but rather because of the effortful component called forth in overcoming an obstacle. One could presume that destructive activity is usually aggressive, but only by reason of the fact that other forces would naturally or inevitably be called into play, opposing the action and setting an obstacle to its accomplishment. Aggression may be destructive, but destructive action need not be aggressive. The same point is reinforced by Parens' (1979) use of the category of nonaggressive destructiveness.

4. Such a motivationally based view of aggression requires certain key distinctions. First there is the distinction between aggression and its accompanying affects. Aggressive acts may be accompanied by a variety of affective states, whether fear, anxiety, lust, love, or even anger and rage. However, an essential note of the present view is that aggression is not defined by its accompanying affects. The intrinsic motivation or purposive dimension of the aggression itself, namely, overcoming an obstacle, whether psychological or physical, is not linked with any specific affective response, but may be connected with a variety of

affective components derived from peripheral or secondary sources. Rage, for example, might be a response to narcissistic injury rather than an expression of aggression. The affective quality of the response has more to do with the stimulus conditions than with eliciting an aggressive response.

5. A second distinction is between aggression and its associated actions. Freud's failure to make this distinction plagued his early thinking about instincts. He regarded instincts as inherently active, that is, as exercising a degree of force on the psychic apparatus. Freud (1915) wrote: "By the pressure of an instinct we understand its motor factor, the amount of force or the measure of the demand for work which it represents. The characteristic of exercising pressure is common to all instincts; it is in fact their very essence. Every instinct is a piece of activity; if we speak loosely of passive instincts, we can only mean instincts whose *aim* is passive" (p. 122).

Review of the Literature

The above formulation of the nature and function of aggression differs from more traditional views of the role of aggression in phobic states. Fenichel (1944) summarized the classic position, in which phobic formations were seen as defenses against both libidinal and aggressive impulses and called into play a variety of defensive processes, including regression, repression, reversal, projection, and displacement. Anna Freud (1977) would later add condensation and externalization.

In general, these formulations attributed the origin of whatever anxiety the phobic phenomenon was defending against to libidinal and aggressive impulses. As Anna Freud (1977) observed, the distinction between anxiety and fear was paramount in that it was not fear that lay at the root of the phobia, but anxiety. The anxieties can reflect any level of developmental danger—annihilation, separation, loss of the object/love, castration, even moral condemnation. They serve essentially as a warning signal against the related intrapsychic danger. While the phobic mechanisms are intended to contain the anxiety within manageable limits so that the internal danger does not become traumatic, the phobic anxiety escapes this containment and the ego is to this extent overwhelmed, but now by an external threat rather than an internal one. Thus, oral sadistic impulses to bite or devour can be transformed into fears of being bitten (Flescher, 1955), sadomasochistic wishes to be beaten and tortured can take the form of fears of dark streets (Brenner, 1959) and other fears of attack or destruction (Bernstein, 1962), murderous wishes against the oedipal father become animal phobias (Freud, 1909; Rochlin, 1973).

The prevailing view of the place of aggression in the formation of phobic processes sees it as a given. The aggressive instinctual drive is an independent source of instinctual danger, in one or other degree reinforced by external factors. In the early classic view, any conjunction with real determinants or situations was not required to explain the phobic phenomenon (e.g., early Kleinian understanding of the death instinct). More recent views would accept a more complex interweaving of developmental and environmental components as integral to any understanding of the vicissitudes of aggression.

A Structural Theory of Aggression in Phobic States

Phobic states are complex compromise formations that involve a number of determining factors. Certain classes of stimuli, for example, seem to be prepotent for eliciting phobic reactions (Marks, 1969, 1970). Phobic reactions to open spaces or travel by train or plane are relatively common, as opposed to phobias of travel by automobile. Some stimuli seem to be more age specific: loud noises or sudden movements trigger fear responses in young infants, stranger anxiety is aroused in somewhat older infants, and animal phobias seem to cluster in preschool children. Fear of open spaces seems to be reserved for adolescence and adulthood. These findings would suggest a role for maturational factors in the genesis of phobic states.

Experience also plays a role. Phase-determining incidents can influence the emergence of dynamic patterns underlying specific phobias. One thinks of separation anxiety in children and animal phobias in the oedipal period. The emergence of animal phobias in children can be elicited by little or no traumatizing episodes, but such a phobia in an adult would require a relatively severe fright or traumatic experience. School and job phobias or, for that matter, in later life, disease and death phobias, involve exposure to the feared situation.

Phobic personalities tend to be timid, shy, dependent, and often immature. Phobias are not restricted to such individuals by any means, but such personalities seem to provide a more fertile soil for phobic disturbances to take root. Phobic patterns can often run in families and can reflect the influence of social and cultural factors (Marks, 1970). Many phobic expressions are relatively limited as a consequence of physical trauma, e.g., fear of dogs after being bitten, fear of heights after a fall, or fear of driving after a car accident. Psychological trauma is usually more difficult to define, but usually is connected with severe anxiety, guilt, or rage. The link between the trauma and the phobic response may not be immediately evident. Agoraphobia may emerge in the wake of a bereavement or loss, marital separation or divorce, an accident, or a life-threatening illness or injury. Long-term phobic reactions are by no means rare in the wake of losses and traumata suffered in catastrophic events (Stern, 1968a,b; Titchener & Kapp, 1976), A phobic response may also serve as a defense against an underlying depression.

I have argued elsewhere (Meissner, 1978) that the mechanisms involved in the genesis of phobic states are similar to those at work in the paranoid process. The phobia is based on the externalization (whether strictly projective or not) by displacement from the inner world of elements of the introjective configuration; it is the displacement of aggressive components that gives the external configuration its phobic effect. In the phobias of childhood, what is defended against and displaced onto the external world is the child's aggressive and destructive impulses. Externalization shades into projection to the extent that the content of the displacement takes on a personal character, specifically to the extent that the displacement reflects a given object derivation. Fear of open spaces is relatively nonobject related; fear of a persecutory object is object connected.

In this sense, Little Hans's (Freud, 1909) phobia of horses leans more in the direction of a projective derivation—in the traditional view, the projection of oral or anal-sadistic impulses transformed into the fear of biting animals. Hostility and sadism were the impulses central to Little Hans's phobia. He wishes his father dead so he would be free to engage in sadistic, phallic acts with his mother and have babies by her. The aggressive motivation came into play by reason of the fact that he saw his father as an obstacle to his access to his mother. Freud thought of the setting of Hans's phobia as a "battle" (p. 139) between opposing forces within the child's mind: impulses of hostility and sadism on one side and repression on the other. According to Freud, Hans's instinctual impulses strove not only to gain ultimate satisfaction, but also to force their way into consciousness. When the instincts were intensified by experiences of deprivation and erotic stimulation, they gained enough force partially to overcome the obstacle of repression. At that point the phobia "burst out" so that previously unconscious ideas "forced their way into consciousness" (p. 139) in the form of fears of horses biting him and horses falling down.

The conflict was essentially oedipal, based on hostility to the father, giving rise to fears of punishment and castration anxiety. The internal psychic danger was translated into an external one, castration anxiety was transformed into phobic anxiety. Biting horses are easier to avoid than castrating fathers. Prior to the emergence of the phobia, repression had protected Hans from feeling hostility toward his father and from experiencing the castration fear that seemed the natural punishment for his forbidden and destructive impulses. When his impulses began to emerge into consciousness, Hans desperately needed adjunctive ways to oppose awareness and expression of them. His phobia served the purpose. His fear of punishment for his impulse to bite his father and see him fall down dead was disguised and externalized as a fear of horses biting him. We can go beyond Freud's interpretation to suggest that this projection also served to reinforce the obstacle to expression of Hans's hostile impulses because it was experienced as a genuine threat; at the same time, it served to maintain a sense of safety and loving relationship with his father, who otherwise would have been the subject of this projection.

Horses falling down were a disguised representation of Hans's desire to penetrate his mother sadistically with his penis and have babies by her. Freud explained the component of fear attached to horses falling down in accordance with ideas about anxiety hysteria he held at that time, i.e., with the return of the repressed the *"the pathogenic material was remodelled and transposed on to the horse-complex, while the accompanying affects were uniformly turned into anxiety"* (p. 137).

In his nightmare, Hans saw himself as a helpless victim. Powerful animals were going to turn on him and hurt him. This fear reflects his unconscious view of his father, but also reflects his sense of his own smallness and weakness—his vulnerability. As Rochlin (1973) has observed, Hans began as an aggressor and ended as the victim. But he also had other resources to deal with his fear. He could play the horse himself and imagine that he could threaten and frighten his father, even bite him. Or he could play the horsemaster and beat the horse to show the horse and himself that he had no fear of him.

The aggressive wish to overcome the obstacle posed by important or loved figures by attacking or harming them becomes in itself a threat—now of the loss of the loved object so attacked. The phobia in part expresses the dread of carrying out the destructive wishes, and thus preserves the intended object of the attack. In both his nightmares and in his waking phobias, Hans became the victim: the aggression toward loved objects became turned against himself. He becomes the victim in order to defend against the threatening aggression against the loved objects. These patterns of aggressive vicissitude reflect the underlying configurations embedded in the introjective organization that lies at the core of Hans's self-organization. The phobic defense operates to repress and displace his sense of himself as destructive aggressor by putting him in the position of the vulnerable, weak and terrorized victim.

Currently, we would add specifically that attaching fear to the sight and expectation of horses falling down would not simply be a disguise of his instinctual aim and a displacement as to object. The fear also compelled him to avoid the possibility of witnessing such an event. We would say that his fear of seeing horses falling down served as an additional obstacle to awareness of and expression of his sadistic incestuous impulses. At the same time, this component of the phobia served as a means for preserving a sense of safety in the presence of his mother, safety from knowing and experiencing forbidden impulses and associated anxiety in relation to her. The phobia also preserved his sense of loving security with her.

In a way that resembles our own thinking, Freud (1909) also viewed the phobia as posing an obstacle to the impulses that were striving toward expression. He wrote:

> . . . the essence of Hans's illness was entirely dependent upon the nature of the instinctual components that had to be repulsed. The content of his phobia was such as to impose a very great measure of restriction upon his freedom of movement, and that was its purpose. It was therefore a powerful reaction against the obscure impulses to movement which were especially directed against his mother. For Hans horses had always typified pleasure in movement. . . ; but since this pleasure in movement included the impulse to copulate, the neurosis posed a restriction on it and exalted the horse into an emblem of terror [p. 139].

Aggression, then, in the phobia of Little Hans was located not in the quality of his affects, nor in the quality of his erotic or hostile impulses, but rather in the interplay of opposing motivations. Prior to the phobia, the striving toward consciousness and satisfaction on the part of his impulses was more or less successfully opposed by the obstacle of repression. Aggression enters the picture to the extent that extra psychic effort may be required to break through the repressive barrier. In addition, insofar as his father posed a threatening obstacle to his desire to possess his mother libidinally, additional aggression would also have come into play with the motive of overcoming and getting rid of this now external obstacle. But the hostile impulse toward his father was also threatening and created a fear of losing father. The aggressive impulses directed at father, in serving to overcome the obstacle posed by the father to his libidinal desires, thus simultaneously became itself an obstacle to a secure, protective and loving relation to his father.

Clinical Examples from Adults

I would like to discuss two cases of phobic formation, one from a psychoanalysis, the other from a brief psychotherapy that lasted about six sessions. My purpose is to focus the role of aggression in the genesis of these phobias. The first case was reported at greater length in a previous study (Meissner et al., 1987).

Paul, a 22-year-old college senior, was asymptomatic until he applied to medical school. He then became increasingly anxious and preoccupied over his admission. After he was accepted, he seemed unable to enjoy his success. Instead, he became more anxious and developed phobic symptoms, especially a fear of contracting syphilis from kissing or even superficial physical contact with girls. He became obsessed with this fear. He also developed a phobia of looking at his penis, fearing that he would find some lesion there—all this even though he had never had sexual relations.

He was concerned about functioning as a physician if he should get syphilis. He reasoned that syphilis affects the brain, makes the individual demented and dangerous, so that he might kill his patients or spread syphilis to the rest of the world so that many would die.

Paul was the older of two boys of a middle-class family; his brother was four years younger. His mother was extremely overprotective, and had raised Paul as her favorite, her "golden boy," and had the highest expectation and hopes for his future. He had previously been able to satisfy his mother's expectations by his achievements. The father was a professional man who also doted on his son. Both parents were very much invested in his becoming a physician.

He had two important memories from childhood. The first was playing with a marionette and in a moment of anger shaking it so hard that he "killed it." The second was a fantasy of himself as Tom Sawyer setting out to find a girlfriend; when he found her, he had tremendous feeling for her, but could not approach her physically in any way.

The patient felt he had always been isolated from the outside world and perceived entering medical school as his introduction to "THE WORLD." In that world, you had to be independent, take care of yourself, compete with others, and take responsibility for peoples' lives, i.e., you could kill them. It also meant having real sex (intercourse) instead of just "making out" or making up stories about having sex. In real sex you could kill the woman "like a marionette."

The analysis revealed a profound fear and hatred of women and of their power to engulf and dominate him. He traced this fear to his mother, who had been greatly idealized by the family, in particular by the father, who spoke of her in adoring terms, as "snow-white pure, a true angel." But the treatment also brought out another side of the mother. She could be extremely sweet, but, if things did not go her way, she could be aloof and removed or, suddenly, she could go into a rage, furiously calling Paul a "dirty bastard." In those moments, which he dreaded, she would turn, in his words, "from an angel into a demon." At those times he was terrified of her and, at the same time, furious but unable to recognize it. Instead, he had frightening thoughts of smashing things or killing people. He connected these thoughts to his memory of "killing" the marionette and to his then unconscious murderous wishes.

He was able to uncover his murderous wishes toward his mother and how he saw her death as the only way to free himself from her oppressive overprotection, her constant fear of his being harmed or his getting sick. At the same time he felt that his father was his only source of affection and was terrified of losing his relationship with his father. The dependent and clinging feelings included bitter resentment at the many times he had wished to go out on his own, to be adventurous like Tom Sawyer, but his parents had prevented him.

He finally was able to go out with girls and even kissed one, and his fear of syphilis diminished, at least to the point of some residual anxiety each time he saw a word starting with 's.' His main phobia persisted. He was still unable to look at his penis out of fear of finding a syphilitic lesion. However, for the first time he began to talk about genitals and how ugly they were, and of how frightened he was of both female and male genitals. He imagined the male organ could certainly kill the woman, that he could kill a woman in sex just as he had killed the marionette when he let himself go as a child. He had a variety of sadistic beating fantasies, along with fears of being killed or maimed himself.

At this point, he had a frightening dream. "I am in the den of my house. There is a table whose top is supported by a single column. Around the column there is a snake coiled. I am not sure if the snake's head was at the top of the column or at the bottom. Next, I wanted to catch the snake which was now coiled around the table on the floor in front of me. I wanted to catch it by the back of the head or the neck. If I could grab him there, he would be unable to turn his head and bite me. I may have been afraid of the snake wrapping around me and squeezing me or strangling me. My mother was present during this part of the dream. She was able to easily grab the snake in the way I wanted to. I wanted to grab the snake so it could not harm me. I may have made some timid and quickly withdrawn attempts. I was pretty sure I couldn't do it. When I looked at it again, it was moving aggressively towards my neck. With the snake near my neck, I became so frightened that I woke up."

He connected this dream with the fear of his mother's affection (squeezing and hugging and kissing him to death) and his fear of sexual intimacy, of killing and being killed. The snake symbol also condensed his ambivalence as a physician and as a young man about to go out into the WORLD, and his need for safety and protection. It also conveyed the fear of his penis and its magical destructive power. He realized how the penis is used to express love and affection and how afraid he was of it all. For the first time he was able to fantasize openly about intercourse, but was still afraid to talk about penetration.

The dream was critical in anticipating the disappearance of his phobia. He finally was able to look at his penis and later to have intercourse with his girlfriend. The other phobic symptoms also vanished. From this point on, the analysis continued to deal with the character problems of a severely obsessive personality.

This medical school phobia has the characteristics of intense, anxiety-provoking, sadistic, murderous, and sexual wishes toward the parents, along with an intense need for parental protection. His conflicts included the fear of his own impulses to do away with the parents who had for so long served as obstacles to his desires to be free. The fear of syphilis protected him from killing or being killed by women. It also protected him against the threat posed by medical school and separation from his parents. The phobia was precipitated by his wish and fear of growing up, leaving home and parents, and beginning to do, now with parental approval, what had been forbidden as a child, i.e., to leave his parents, go out into the world, and have sex.

What, then, are the components of his intrapsychic conflict? Like Little Hans, hostility and sadism are the impulses central to the patient's pathology. Since childhood, he had wished his parents and his brother dead, and thus to be an orphan and free like Tom Sawyer. He was convinced of his physical power to kill because he had "killed" the marionette. His defense against these wishes took the form of docile obedience reinforced by severe obsessive defenses: reaction formation and isolation of affect. His admission to medical school, however, forced his sadistic impulses to consciousness. Now he had to leave home, have sex, face the world and the grownups, and stop being a child—in short he had to renounce the passive security that had reinforced the repression of his sadistic sexual and murderous impulses. Repression gave way to intense murderous and sexually sadistic impulses, the return of the repressed. The fear of looking at his penis—the murderous weapon—protected him against further awareness of his rage against destructive women. The fear of syphilis protected him against full awareness of his situation, i.e., the feeling of being betrayed by his parents and the concomitant murderous anger toward them. The phobia was an expression of the fear of the punishment he deserved for his impulses as well as protection against the threat of having to leave home.

The second case was a woman in her early 30s who suffered from severe agoraphobia. Her history contained no significant previous psychiatric morbidity, and her visit to my office was her first contact with a psychiatrist. She was an intelligent, psychologically minded, and well-motivated patient. Her symptoms were severe and she had been housebound for about a year and a half. She could not leave the house, could not even step out on the front porch without severe anxiety and a sense of panic. The attacks were marked by severe anxiety, heart pounding, inability to breathe, sweating, and a sense of doom—as though she were going to die. Her social life had become extremely constricted and the burdens on her family considerable. She was able to visit her mother who lived next door if someone took her the few steps across the yard. She could also go shopping if her husband was with her, not without anxiety, but without the desperate panic and fear of dying. She was able to get to my office only because her husband brought her, a burden to him because he had to forgo work time with a consequent loss of income.

She engaged readily and easily in the treatment, formed from the beginning a positive and well-motivated alliance. The story quickly unfolded. She had been the middle child of three daughters spaced roughly two years apart. The oldest girl was a behavioral problem, rebellious, resentful, angry, with a fair degree of school difficulties, and constantly at loggerheads with the parents. The youngest girl had cerebral palsy, which was not so much a severe impairment as a source of constant preoccupation and anxious concern for the parents, especially the mother. My patient was the relatively untroubled middle child, did well in school, never a behavioral problem, rarely sick or troubled, compliant and obedient, constantly concerned to please her mother and to try to be helpful to mother who was so burdened and troubled by the other two daughters. Not surprisingly, it did not take much uncovering to reach the resentment and disappointment she had felt as a child at always having to take a back seat to her sisters, always giving way to their needs or demands, feeling like a second-class citizen and that she had to work hard and sacrifice much to gain any recognition or affection from her mother.

My patient had pursued her education through junior college and then worked for several years as a secretary. She then married and moved to another city with her husband. She had two children, a boy and a girl, and seemed happily married and content. After a few years, for several reasons they decided to move back to her home town, and in fact moved into the house next to her own family home where her mother still lived, her father having died several years previously. It was soon after this move that the phobic symptoms began to express themselves.

The therapy took the form of my actively exploring with her the pattern of events and their meaning. She was able to respond productively to my prompting with useful memories and associations. We also arranged a systematic schedule of desensitizing steps that were discussed, planned, and carried out by her quite effectively. I saw her once weekly, and she would discuss her progress and the difficulties she encountered week by week. As the exploration into the meaning of her symptoms progressed, she continued to make steady progress in tolerating and overcoming the phobic anxiety and gradually extending the range of her activities outside the house. She was greatly relieved and encouraged by her evident progress.

I present the salient factors that emerged from our discussions, so as to make a short story shorter. To begin, Mother was herself phobic and had been so for many years. She was also house bound. If my patient wanted to see her mother, she had to go over to mother's house. The return home and the decision to move in next door to mother reactivated a variety of unconscious infantile wishes in my patient. Her need to seek acceptance and approval from mother was uppermost. Mother's seeming disregard for the patient, and her greater involvement with the patient's sisters concretely took the form of her mother's attitudes toward her children. She paid more attention and was more generous with her sisters' children than with the patient's children. The mother would not visit them, of course, but even though they lived next door, the mother never made any effort to invite, entertain, or babysit with the children. Any times that my patient had to call on the mother to take care of the children for her, it felt like an imposition and my patient would end up wishing that she had never asked.

It was not hard to put the pieces of the puzzle together. The move back and the resulting proximity to mother activated old infantile yearnings to gain mother's love and approval. But just as in the old days, that yearning ran afoul of mother's indifference and selfishness, and her preferential treatment of the other daughters. This did not seem to be altogether a distortion on the part of my patient, in that mother continued to feel that the sisters needed her help and attention more than my patient who as a rule seemed very well able to fend for herself. Another element was some resentment on the mother's part that my patient had gone off with her husband and abandoned the mother, a move toward independence and autonomy that did not sit well with the needy and controlling part of the mother.

The phobia found a way to articulate itself into this picture with a variety of overdetermined motivations. In one respect, the phobia played out the patient's identification with the mother, bringing to the fore the victim elements that seemed to play such a central role in the mother's pathology and formed the core of the identification with the victimized mother. This way a way of achieving some sense of union with the mother—they were joined in their affliction. Thus the patient could elicit sympathy and acceptance from the mother in a way that her healthy and independent stance would not allow. The phobia allowed her to outdo the neediness of the sisters, and put an even greater claim on mother's concern and attention.

And what about the role of aggression? I would see the aggression as tied up with the rivalry and competition with the sisters, particularly for the mother's love. Her rage at the sisters was considerable, stemming from very early levels, but continuing into adult life. Her anger was directed at the mother as well, for her preferential treatment of the sisters and for denying my patient the closeness and acceptance she so desperately sought. The objective here was to gain a closer relationship with the mother, and the obstacles to be overcome were the mother's indifference and the preference for the sisters. The rage at mother and sisters could not be directly expressed because that would only frustrate her goal and further defeat her need for acceptance from the mother. The phobia came into the service of the patient's aggressive drive to overcome these obstacles on one side; on another side, the aggression that was so frustrated in its expression against the offending objects was displaced and externalized into the phobic symptom, specifically into the threat and anxiety experienced in going out of the house, the model for which was set by the mother's phobia and the wish to identify with the mother. Some other phobia or some other set of symptoms would not have served half as well, since the best appeal to mother's sympathy lie in the reproduction of her own pattern of symptoms. And on a third side, the aggressive conflicts in the patient would not allow much room for the tolerance of aggressive impulses, so that her defensive need to counter and avoid the aggression and associated rage she felt required that she adopt the position of the suffering victim rather than to see herself as a destructive or hostile aggressor. The symptomatic expression of the phobia interacted with and reflected the shift to the dominance of victim introject that was being enacted in the development of the symptom.

The treatment lasted only a few weeks, due in large measure to the patient's ability to focus on the relevant material and to assimilate in useful ways the understanding that she developed in the course of our investigation. As this understanding emerged, she was increasingly able to reestablish a more realistic and adaptive stance and to come to terms with the difficulties in her relationship with the mother and to reconcile herself to the inevitable disappointments. This understanding abetted her efforts to gradually modify her phobic fears and behavior. The whole treatment consumed only a few weeks. Subsequently, the patient resurfaced after about a year and a half with a recrudescence of her phobic symptoms. We were quickly able to identify the precipitating events that again had to do with a disappointment from mother; as before the symptoms cleared after two sessions, and I have not heard from her for nearly a decade.

A Model of Phobia and Aggression

A phobia is a symptom deriving from intrapsychic conflict. The manifest affect dominating the symptom is anxiety. What gives rise to the anxiety is not dynamically significant in itself, but rather as an object of symbolic displacement and externalization of an intolerable mental conflictual content. The phobia is a compromise formation that makes this psychic situation relatively more tolerable. The compromise involves simultaneously contradictory motivations: on one hand to gain access to an object or goal of libidinal or narcissistic investment, and on the other to avoid the intrapsychic danger posed by its attainment. The phobia creates an element of safety in a context assessed as dangerous by displacing and externalizing one of the conflictual components. The dangers against which the phobia defend are the classic psychic dangers—castration, loss of the object, loss of love, or loss of self-esteem. The more profound fear of loss of a sense of self, or self-cohesion or annihilation anxiety strikes at a more fundamental level that lies more deeply than the issues of conflict. As a generalization, we could say that these are dangers which threaten to disturb the subjective state of well-being. These dangers present an obstacle to the maintenance of well-being in terms of body narcissism, object attachment, secondary narcissism, and ego-superego equilibrium.

Although the phobic symptom may include the avoidance of particular situations and things, the phobic structure does not include any external action on the part of the individual. Even when reality may pose some threat to the phobic individual, should one of the forbidden wishes be expressed, this is not the significant danger. The dangers that contribute to the formation of a phobia are entirely intrapsychic.

Aggression in the formation of a phobia involves not only the effort to overcome an external obstacle, whether person, thing, or situation, but more particularly may involve an effort to overcome internal psychic obstacles. In ordinary psychoanalytic language, this activity is involved in the organization of psychic defenses. Anna Freud graphically illustrates the aggressive nature of the defenses when she describes the appearance of resistance in following the fundamental rule: "This means that the inroad of the id into the ego has given place to a counterattack by the ego upon the id" (1936, p. 14). The intrapsychic battle lines are drawn and "Were it not for the intervention of the ego, or of those external forces which the ego represents, every instinct would know only one fate—that of gratification" (p. 44).

We would argue that aggression comes into play only at that point at which an action or state of psychic equilibrium is inhibited, impeded, or otherwise countered by an obstacle. Any mental process, from an image to a thought or fantasy, to an impulse, or to some form of motivation, can serve as an obstacle. Aggression in this general sense in the formation of defenses may take the form of creating or imposing a barrier or countering mechanism opposing the unimpeded expression of an instinctual drive; or the free imposition of superego standards, prohibitions, or punishments; or the conscious acknowledgment of a dreaded (fantasied or real) interpersonal situation. Such a defense mechanism is aggressive insofar as it is called into play when the unimpeded expression of the drive or other psychic force would create an obstacle or impediment to other psychic aims or objectives (usually but not exclusively associated with the ego). In this sense Hans's impulse to hurt his father, motivated by the need to eliminate the obstacle he posed to Hans's libidinal desires for his mother, interfered with and imposed an obstacle to his loving attachment to his father. The defensive displacement of his impulse from his father onto the horse involved the use of aggression in order to overcome this latter obstacle, which carried with it the threat of the loss of the father or his love. Aggression, by the same token, can also come into play when an additional degree of effort or intensity is required for the drive to gain expression or attain its object. In the face of a defensive barrier, whether repressive or otherwise, an additional degree of intensity or effort may be mobilized as a consequence of motivation to overcome the defensive obstacle and gain satisfaction.

This description suggests that aggression is frequently at work in ordinary psychic life. In normal circumstances it operates silently and unobtrusively, aiming at maintaining adequate psychic satisfaction and functioning. Aggression becomes overt and behaviorally obvious when the obstacle posed to some motivation requires overt action on external objects or some other form of behavioral expression, or when the affective component that accompanies the behavior becomes manifest. However, aggression may be neither overt nor behaviorally obvious as is often the case in phobic symptom formation.

Seen in this perspective, a phobia may be conceptualized as the final result of a series of defensive maneuvers to overcome a situation in which incompatible needs or wishes and their anticipatory fantasized actions can be neither resolved nor renounced. Each wish and its derivatives pose an obstacle to the fulfillment of the opposing wishes. In the example of the agoraphobic woman, her wishes to be passively dependent and loved were set in opposition to the destructive wish to hurt and destroy her mother and sisters. The passive side creates an obstacle to any more assertive and self-sufficient adulthood, while the destructive wishes stand in the way of comfortable passivity and dependency. The phobia creates an obstacle to separateness even as it works to remove those obstacles that stand in the patient's way to gaining a closer and more loving relationship with her mother. The compromise underlying the symptom formation locked her into a position of continuing infantile dependence that was frustrated and opposed by the mother's indifference or preference for the sisters.

Alternatively, one obstacle posed by one wish (e.g., the wish to retaliate against the mother) is overcome by the first level of defense, the repression of the idea. Repression is at the service of preventing representational awareness, which, once achieved, requires that the represented satisfaction be obtained, compelling the subject to act. This conscious representation becomes in and of itself an obstacle. To remove it aggression draws on the defensive maneuver of repression. The other side of the wish brings the repressed material back to consciousness.

The next level of defense is the disguise of the idea by displacement onto an apparently innocent object, in this case the outside world, that is, the world outside of mother's presence. The wish persists and reappears in relation to the object of displacement which now has to be avoided. The defenses do not work properly because the ambivalent nature of the wish does not permit full repression. Each new aggressive-defensive move against a wish that in its present form cannot be renounced and therefore has become a new obstacle creates the need for further aggressive internal action to overcome the obstacle that refuses to disappear. Finally, a significant portion of the subjects has to be constricted to keep the intrapsychic dangers repressed, and to substitute for them a more tolerable and manageable external threat.

The analysis of the role of aggression in conflict-and-defense with regard to phobia formation deals primarily with conflicts of defense. The same analysis may not be equally applicable to all contexts of conflict, e.g., conflicts of ambivalence (Kris, 1984). Conflicts of ambivalence involve divergent rather than convergent opposites, and are resolved through mourning rather than aggressive action. In such conflicts aggression would not be involved in the internal dynamics of the conflict as such. The conflict may pose an obstacle to other objectives, e.g., resistance to free association, and may thus elicit an aggressive response.

This view of aggression in the psychic formation of a phobia permits a developmental and dynamic understanding of the vicissitudes and interplay of contradictory needs and the progressive and aggressively motivated defensive efforts aimed at maintaining psychic balance and self-protection. The symptom of phobia formation emerges as the result of a progressive narrowing of choices, which forces the individual to resort to condensation and externalization as final defenses (after attempts at regression, repression, reversal, projection, and displacement). These two defenses condense in a particular object or circumstance the motivation to fulfill a variety of unmanageable wishes and locate them external to the self. In this way, even when the phobia elicits intense anxiety, the sense of self is protected and self-equilibrium may be maintained.

Certain individuals seem to be more prone to phobia formation than others. I would suggest that the dynamics of phobia formation reach beyond issues of mere drive-and-defense, that they impinge on more persistent characterological and structural levels of personality organization. Individuals whose constitution and character formation have dealt poorly with the developmental vicissitudes of aggression so that the internalization of aggressive derivatives has been inadequately effected, may be more likely to resort to the defensive processes that culminate in phobia formation. In terms of my own view of the paranoid process (Meissner, 1978, 1981, 1986), phobia formation is another expression of the victim-introject which not only acts to defend against and resolve aggressive conflicts, but also represents a more-or-less constant characterological formation at the core of the individual's sense of self. The sense of self as victim may often underlie and reinforce the mechanisms of phobia formation. This underlying self-configuration may provide a matrix of vulnerability for dealing with aggressive derivatives in symptomatic phobia formation.

REFERENCES

Bernstein, I. (1962). Dreams and masturbation in an adolescent boy. *J. Amer. Psychoanal. Assn.*, 10:289–302.

Brenner, C. (1959). The masochistic character: Genesis and treatment. *J. Amer. Psychoanal. Assn.*, 7:197–226.

Buie, D. H., Meissner, W. W., Rizzuto, A. M., & Sashin, J. I. (1983). Aggression in the psychoanalytic situation. *Int. Rev. Psychoanal.*, 10:159–170.

Fenichel, O. (1944). Remarks on the common phobias. In *The Collected Papers of Otto Fenichel,* second series. New York: Norton, 1954, pp. 278–287.

Flescher, J. (1955). A dualistic viewpoint on anxiety. *J. Amer. Psychoanal. Assn.*, 3:415–446.

Freud, A. (1936). *The Ego and the Mechanisms of Defense. Writings,* Vol. 1. New York: Int. Univ. Press.

_____ (1977). Fears, anxieties, and phobic phenomena. *Psychoanal. Study Child,* 32:85–90.

Freud, S. (1909). Analysis of a phobia in a five-year-old boy. *S.E.*, 10.

_____ (1915). Instincts and their vicissitudes. *S.E.*, 14.

Klein, G. S. (1967). Peremptory ideation: Structure and force in motivated ideas. In *Motives and Thought: Psychoanalytic Essays in Honor of David Rapaport,* ed. R. R. Holt. Psycholog. Issues, Monogr. 18/19. New York: Int. Univ. Press, pp. 80–128.

Kris, A. O. (1984). The conflicts of ambivalence. *Psychoanal. Study Child,* 39:213–234.

Laplanche, J., & Pontalis, J.-B. (1973). *The Language of Psychoanalysis.* New York: Norton.

Marks, I. M. (1969). *Fears and Phobias.* New York: Academic Press.

_____ (1970). The origins of phobic states. *Amer. J. Psychother.*, 24:652–676.

Meissner, W. W. (1978). *The Paranoid Process.* New York: Jason Aronson.

_____ (1981). *Internalization in Psychoanalysis. Psycholog. Issues, Monogr.* 50. New York: Int. Univ. Press.

_____ (1986). *Psychotherapy and the Paranoid Process.* Northvale, NJ: Jason Aronson.

_____ Rizzuto, A. M., Sashin, J. I., & Buie, D. H. (1987). A view of aggression in phobic states. *Psychoanal. Q.*, 56:452–476.

Parens, H. (1979). *The Development of Aggression in Early Childhood.* New York: Jason Aronson.

Rochlin, G. (1973). *Man's Aggression: The Defense of the Self.* Boston: Gambit.

Stern, M. (1968a). Fear of death and trauma. *Int. J. Psychoanal.*, 49:458–461.

_____ (1968b). Fear of death and neurosis. *J. Amer. Psychoanal. Assn.*, 16:3–31.

Titchener, J. L., & Kapp, F. T. (1976). Family and character change at Buffalo Creek. *Amer. J. Psychiat.*, 133:295–299.

129 Mount Auburn Street
Cambridge, MA 02138

Challenge, Apraxia, and Avoidance

JOHN E. GEDO, M.D.

A MAN IN HIS LATE 30S, in the eighth year of an analysis undertaken because of paralyzing difficulties in love and work that had driven him to despair, managed at long last to fall in love for the first time. Contrary to his invariable habit in relation to the countless women he had discarded in a career of Don Juanism, he was not preoccupied with listing the alleged shortcomings of his inamorata's status or prestige. In fact, he was almost craven in his tolerance of her initial lack of commitment to their relationship, and he refrained entirely from raising objections to her behavior and preferences, although he often found these rather difficult to bear. Only certain dreams of vengeance on a woman (in the manifest content, this was sometimes explicitly his mother)—especially revenge by means of sexual infidelities—betrayed the fact that he was enraged by these deprivations and once again on the verge of lapsing into the guerrilla warfare that had characterized his dealings with his parents for over three decades.

In these circumstances, I predicted a rupture of this important relationship—the first contingency to have relieved the patient's chronic depressive mood—unless he could make his needs clear to his beloved and gain her cooperation in mitigating his dissatisfactions. Although he was in complete agreement with this pessimistic forecast, the patient could not mobilize himself to discuss these

Dr. Gedo recently retired as a Training and Supervisory Analyst, Chicago Institute for Psychoanalysis. He is the author of a number of books, the most recent of which is *The Mind in Disorder*.

matters with the frustrator. Instead of taking such action, he spent a number of analytic sessions in obsessive rehearsals of how she would fend off and/or rebut whatever he might call to her attention. This behavior was an exact repetition of his response, relatively early in the analysis, to the need to confront his father about certain financial arrangements between them that no longer suited the patient. He had avoided that confrontation for a long time, ostensibly in fear of his father's expectable hostile reactions. When, after many delays, he had broached the matter in a series of letters, the issue was resolved amicably, and the patient's projective distortions about his father's attitudes toward him were gradually corrected.

Based on this precedent, I became aware of the fact that the patient's willingness to sacrifice his first loving relationship to a woman amounted to a phobic avoidance of a potential negotiation between them. Consequently, I pointed out that he had no right to put hostile arguments into her mouth; moreover, as the transaction with his father had shown us, it was quite probable that the only hostility in play was his own. Although he continued to postpone action in the hope of some magical solution, the patient did acknowledge that his lover was evidently unaware of his objections to some of her behavior and was likely to be devastated if he abandoned her, as he was now tempted to do.

Not at all coincidentally, it was on Valentine's day that he finally overcame his reluctance to clear the air between them. He opened his session the next morning with a highly distressed account of how incompetent he had been in bringing his objections to her attention. He barely acknowledged in passing that she had been quite accommodating in her response and had only objected to his failure to state his requirements promptly and candidly. Although the interpersonal problem had evaporated, he now felt much worse about the humiliation of having shown himself to be unable to communicate adequately about relatively simple human transactions. What was worse, his lover had revealed that her own failure to discuss their evolving relationship was caused by her dislike of his manner of discourse. Although, needless to say, she did not use technical terms to describe this, she had accurately pinpointed his obsessional vagueness, his inability to deal with emotions, and his tendency to miss the point when she was not talking in ways intended to be taken literally. The fact that their colloquium had promoted the relationship and prevented a needless rupture did not console the patient for this humiliating revelation of his limitations.

The man whose phobic behavior I have just described, all too briefly, possessed the Pride of Lucifer or, if you will, was a Monster of Vanity. When he started his analysis, he had dreams of walking in ceremonial processions, clad in capes the size of a football field. Of course it was the priority he always gave to status and prestige (to be more accurate, the priority these had acquired when his initial love for his mother had curdled under the impact of her truly cruel disregard for his needs) that led to his disastrous policy of avoiding potential humiliations. Yet we would be unjustified if we disregarded his claim that the avoidance of confrontations also served to forestall certain anxieties—castration fear in relation to his father and fear of loss of love with his lady friend—for he was just as limited in his capacity to deal with an upsurge of affect as he was handicapped in discussions of emotional transactions. In other words, any outbreak of anxiety was likely to humiliate him as well.

The probable connection of phobic avoidances with an inability to deal with mounting affect (anxiety) was also noted by Kohut (1984, pp. 28–32) in the specific instance of agoraphobia: he postulated that this syndrome, which is generally mitigated in the presence of a familiar person, betokens an inability to soothe oneself. This suggested explanation properly distinguishes between the cause of the anxiety in question (let us say, as traditional interpretations would have it, the sexual temptations of the agora) and that of the final symptom, the phobic avoidance. In his brief excursus on this subject, Kohut failed to consider why many people find it intolerable to *experience* unrelieved anxiety, even if this choice leads to crippling self-restrictions. Nor did he address the question whether analogous disabilities in self-regulation may lie behind phobias unrelieved by the availability of human assistance.

As the clinical illustration with which I began suggests, one possible link between deficits in self-regulation and a policy of avoidance (i.e., the establishment of a phobia) is an inability to accommodate to circumstances understood as humiliations. In my clinical experience with the psychoanalytic method, I have encountered no other linkages of this kind, although this does not mean of course that they do not exist. At any rate, for the time being, we can postulate that, in childhood, if such intolerance for humiliation does not stand in the way, deficits in autoregulatory capacities will be overcome through the educational efforts of the caretakers. The response of my patient's lover to his mastery of the phobic behavior constitutes the first step in his reeducation (to use Freud's term, *Nacherziehung*): she instructed him in the precise nature of the psychological skills he needed to acquire. As I have stated elsewhere (1988, Epilogue), one way to conceptualize psychoanalysis-as-treatment is to regard it as a technology of such remedial education in a series of missing skills (ego deficits I prefer to call *apraxias*).

In psychoanalytic practice, I have observed a wide variety of avoidant behaviors caused by the foregoing dynamic constellation. For instance, one man entirely avoided social relations with women for several decades because he was afraid that if he attempted sexual relations he might humiliate himself because of a need to inhibit certain perverse inclinations. Neither did he have the capacity to channel his sexual excitement by interposing a layer of fantasy between his interpersonal transactions and his subjective experience, nor could he negotiate mutual accommodation with a potential sexual partner. Be it noted that the avoidance of women did not supervene until well past adolescence, a period during which this man unselfconsciously acted out his perverse impulses. His horizons subsequently expanded, and his standards of behavior were markedly raised by his gradual absorption of upper middle-class values; his behavior became phobic only when he lost his shamelessness.

At the opposite extreme we find cases of the infernal pride I noted in the young man who dreamt of being the star of princely ceremonials. One such person, who was the favored child of a schizophrenic mother with megalomanic ideas, led a life of schizoid withdrawal in order to avoid ordinary human experiences, for these had humiliating connotations for him—like Shakespeare's Bottom, he expected himself to be vastly superior to mere mortals, as his mother had indicated he was. When explanations of this kind challenged this man to attempt to overcome his avoidance of social relations, he was initially so clumsy that he did, in fact, embarrass himself on various occasions. It was noteworthy that these trivial *faux pas* enraged him at me because he held me responsible for exposing him to potentially humiliating situations. In other words, he was of the character type Kohut (1971) singled out as the "narcissistic personality disorder."

So-called counterphobic behaviors may be understood to be caused by very similar preferences to preserve false pride at the expense of adaptation; they might be termed instances of "there is nothing to be ashamed of but fear itself." Viewed in this way, these patterns of action actually constitute veritable phobias, and the term *counterphobic* for them is a misnomer. In other words, the mastery of a counterphobic pattern is contingent on a lowering of false pride and does not risk the emergence of an *avoidance* of the action that was previously engaged in compulsively. For example, one patient who rushed in where angels fear to tread in attempting to keep crazy women happy was enacting a grandiose fantasy he needed for complex reasons referable to his situation in early childhood. When we succeeded in clarifying these issues in the analysis, he divorced his psychotic spouse, but this sensible course of action did not render him fearful about holding his own with her or with other crazy people. It makes good sense to understand the clinical gain in this case as the mastery of a phobic avoidance of the shameful status of a "quitter."

All of the cases I have cited thus far actually conform to the hypothesis put forward by Moraitis (1988) to the effect that what the phobic person is actually avoiding is a situation of novelty. Because Moraitis is mainly concerned with a theory of knowledge, his hypothesis is focused on mental contents, and in those terms it seems to be entirely correct. For my patient the Prince, it was the effort to understand the subjectivity of a beloved person that was unprecedented; for the person with perverse sexuality, it would have been the requirement to put the needs of another ahead of his own wishes; for the schizoid patient, it was social relations of a conventional kind; for the "counterphobic" man, it was the acknowledgment that he was vulnerable to the disruptions caused by his crazy wife. The common denominator in every instance is the inability of each person to deal successfully with the new challenge in an age-appropriate manner. In other words, Moraitis has a valid insight that can best be turned to account if we focus on the fact that novelty represents an adaptive challenge that calls for the deployment of manifold psychological capacities.

I am well aware of the fact that the illustrative material I have presented consists entirely of cases wherein the situation feared and avoided is directly discernible, in contrast to the conventional examples of phobia which are complicated by displacement of the fear onto a symbol. The classic case is that of the zoophobia of Little Hans (Freud, 1909), a boy in an oedipal crisis whose ambivalence toward his father and fears of retaliation were condensed in the fear of being attacked by a horse and a consequent avoidance of going into the street. I have chosen illustrative cases without this superimposition of defensive distortion precisely to facilitate understanding by focusing on the simplest of instances.

I believe, however, that a childhood zoophobia also needs to be understood in terms of a fear of self-regulatory failure—although, in the oedipal period, the inability to contain anxiety without resort to defensive operations (the apraxia Freud [1926] called the "actual neurotic core" of a neurosis, i.e., the propensity to be overwhelmed by affect) is still more or less age-appropriate. Nonetheless, I would assume that if this deficit is severe enough to lead to the formation of a childhood neurosis in the shape of a phobia, as it did in the case of Little Hans, the child must be attempting to avoid the repeated humiliation of experiencing mounting anxiety without the resources to cope with it.

It is well to recall in this connection that childhood zoophobias tend to be self-limiting; in latency, they are generally folded into a character neurosis, often of an obsessional type. Such a solution is contingent on a regression to more primitive fantasy systems—in the case of obsessional personalities, to fantasies of an anal-sadistic variety. Another way to view the substitution of a deformation of character for a preexisting phobia is to recall the common finding that in the course of analyzing neurotic characters, the advent of a full-blown transference neurosis may be heralded by the emergence of the affect connected to a long-forgotten zoophobia. These commonplaces of developmental psychology may be more understandable if we keep in mind that the choice of the phobic symptom is dictated by the child's immaturity in terms of mastering anxiety. (This is why we can assure analysands that, in adulthood, they should be able to "work through" a transference neurosis involving the very same conflicts that defeated them as children.) The return of derivatives of the childhood symptom in the course of analysis betokens the voluntary relaxation of the defenses originally used to fend it off; what we then call the process of working through consists of the gradual acquisition of self-regulatory capacities in the face of anxiety. Moreover, in most cases the reemergence of the childhood fear does not compel the adult analysand to engage in *avoidances*—it is much more usual to experience the repetition in the form of anxiety dreams. We help the working through process by teaching analysands that their own emotions will not hurt them—not of course by making pronouncements to that effect, but through arranging for the analysand to experience that he or she can live through these affective storms simply by tolerating them as they naturally occur in the course of analysis.

If it should be granted that the avoidance of the symbol for a situation of danger does not differ in principle from a direct avoidance of such a threat, what, then, constitutes the essential distinction between Little Hans and the various Little Princes I have described here? The most direct answer to this question involves the point implicit in the pun I have just used: Little Hans apparently saw himself as an ordinary little boy full of silly ideas; my analysands, in contrast, were full of grandiose notions of their extraordinary worth and suprahuman capacities. While Hans was struggling with the putative dangers of retaliation for his oedipal hostilities, Little Princes are threatened by a potential disillusionment concerning their status and prestige. *Pari passu,* the defenses typically brought into play in these distinctive circumstances are also different: as Freud's follow-up almost two decades after the child's treatment revealed, Little Hans resolved the affair by obliterating its memory—i.e., repression proper supervened. In each of the cases I have cited, it was disavowal that carried the primary burden of defense: relevant memories from childhood were freely available for recall, but their significance was not acknowledged.

In terms of the hierarchical model of psychic functioning first put forward in my collaboration with Goldberg (Gedo & Goldberg, 1973; see also Gedo, 1979, 1988), the conditions characteristic of the childhood neurosis of Little Hans are collectively designated as Mode IV, which is age-appropriate for an oedipal child. The capacity to make use of symbolization and displacement as additional defensive operations is an equally expectable part of the cognitive armamentarium at this age level. By contrast, the mental dispositions I have attributed to the analysands I describe here characterize Mode III in the hierarchical schema. The fact that these analysands failed to make use of the age-appropriate symbolic capacities that eventually became available to them in order to disguise the real issues they needed to avoid betrays the relatively archaic origin of their difficulties: their defensive posture became structured prior to the secure acquisition of these cognitive skills.

It is the ability to master the "actual neurotic core" produced by a severe intrapsychic conflict that marks the passage from Mode IV to Mode V, that of expectable adult functioning. In other words, when a person learns to regulate his own affective reactions without external assistance and without resort to defensive distortions, there is no further need for symptom formation. At the other end of the developmental scale, do we encounter phobias even more archaic in structure than those I have placed in the category of Mode III? Although individuals whose usual level of functioning is in Mode II are unable to cope outside of a sheltered environment, we do occasionally treat analytic patients who generally function on a higher level but demonstrate the continuing influence of a split-off nucleus of mentation organized in a maximally primitive manner. In order to facilitate the consideration of this topic, I shall briefly present some data from such a case. (I have previously discussed other aspects of this analysis; see Gedo [1981, chap. 7, case 15].)

This analysand also lived the life of a Prince—roughly in the manner of the Student Prince of operetta fame—but he was haunted by a disabling obsessional symptom, a preoccupation with the possibility that he might not be able to continue breathing. If he did not have a therapist available, in a manner analogous to an iron lung, this anxiety about the absence of self-regulation (concretized in terms of a single physiological function) began to verge on panic; consequently, he had been in more or less continuous therapy since late adolescence. This state of affairs was established when the nursemaid who had raised him since early childhood definitely retired; a few years earlier, when she had first thought of leaving, there was a briefer premonitory outbreak of the same hypochondriacal syndrome.

During the regime of the reliable nursemaid, the only obvious sign of the presence of serious psychopathology was a water phobia, which persisted through the patient's latency. To be more precise, this was an avoidance of occasions when the boy was expected to go swimming; the anxiety implicit in these situations was that he might drown, or, to put it in a way that connects this symptom with the hypochondriacal one that succeeded it, that he would be prevented from breathing. The symptom was most prominent when the boy was sent away to summer camp, i.e., when the availability of his nursemaid was in some question. It was not entirely clear just when the phobia started, but it does not seem likely that opportunities to go swimming presented themselves much before latency.

On the basis of the analytic work, we arrived at the conclusion that the fear of drowning was, for this man, an echo of earlier fears of succumbing to the pull for symbiotic fusion with an enormously seductive, intrusive, egocentric, and infantile mother. During the oedipal period, the boy was made to feel that he was the most important person in her orbit; this privileged position entailed the responsibility of meeting her infinite emotional demands—a situation in which he certainly felt out of his depth. It was against the seductive pull of this dangerous liaison that the prosaic but commonsensical nursemaid provided an effective counterweight. To put it in a different way, when the boy was allowed to live out the grandiose fantasy of being his mother's lover, his inability to keep her sufficiently satisfied to prevent her from getting depressed threatened at all times traumatically to deflate him. (These issues were relived in the analytic transference with the roles reversed—i.e., he played the part of his childhood mother, and he tried to make me feel helpless and inadequate, as he had been made to feel when he was invited into her bed.)

The water phobia constituted a childhood neurosis wherein the symptom made use of a minimal displacement by way of the concretization of the subjective fantasy of being helpless, unsupported, overwhelmed. In this sense, water did not constitute an abstract symbol of the engulfing mother; rather, the putative sensation of drowning served as a concrete analogue for the quality of the mother-child relationship. I make the assumption that this equivalence was established in the oedipal period on the basis of prior transactions that did not permit this child to maintain his independent volition vis-à-vis his tyrannical mother.

It should be noted that the maternal grandmother was on the scene for the first two years of the patient's life and apparently served as an alternative to the mother, as the nursemaid (hired when the grandmother unexpectedly died) was to do afterward. Thus, from the dawn of consciousness, this child had two sets of experiences that could not be integrated with each other—neither could be labeled "true" or "false," à la Winnicott (1955), but there remained a cleavage between them in the manner familiar to us from cases in which those labels apply.

If my reconstructions in this case were valid (a hypothesis supported but not substantiated by the excellent therapeutic outcome), it follows that the phobia, established because of the unmanageable anxieties stirred up by the Phyrrhic victory of the oedipal child, was operative in a segment of mental life seemingly structured in a manner expectable in Mode IV. However, this arrangement of psychic dispositions could only be maintained with external support; when such assistance was unavailable, a much more primitive aspect of functioning became manifest, that of a severe hypochondriasis. This state corresponds to Mode II in the hierarchical schema, most clearly because of the coexistence of differently structured nuclei of function, one hypochondriacal, the other self-observing. The hypochondriacal preoccupation is a desperate effort to ward off the threat of disintegration into total confusion (see Gedo, 1979, pp. 210–213). In a certain sense, even its manifest content ("I cannot control my breathing"), cries from the rooftops that self-regulation is out of the question. When this state of desperate disrepair is covered over by a relationship that amounts to a covert symbiosis, the phobic symptom serves as a warning signal of the dangers implicit in giving in to the temptations of grandiose enterprises.

Of course, in this case, as in that of my other Princes, improvement was contingent on curbing the presumption of claiming to be able to accomplish the impossible, a grandiosity that also constituted an identification with the mother's megalomania. A metaphoric way to put the patient's dilemma is that he was ever in danger of drowning in his mother's craziness unless a very sober person held him back from jumping into that deep water. In this instance, therefore, the daunting challenge to be overcome was not that of novelty but of the potentialities inherent in regression to the most archaic modes of functioning within the patient's behavioral repertory. Hence this illustration conforms to the explanation Kohut (1971) offered for the acrophobias: he postulated that those who are afraid of heights are tempted to enact the grandiose fantasy of being able to fly. In this sense, both acrophobia and the water phobia I have described constitute adaptive responses to the potential activation of a "psychotic core" in the depths. The reality ego rightly says, "Get thee behind me, Satan!"

Phobias, like people, are more complex than we like to believe. And there is no way to predict which challenges a person may experience he may feel shamefully unprepared to meet.

REFERENCES

Freud, S. (1909). Analysis of a phobia in a five-year-old boy. *S.E.,* 10.

______ (1926). Inhibitions, symptoms and anxiety. *S. E.,* 20.

Gedo, J. (1979). *Beyond Interpretation.* New York: Int. Univ. Press.

______ (1981). *Advances in Clinical Psychoanalysis.* New York: Int. Univ. Press.

______ (1988). *The Mind in Disorder.* Hillsdale, NJ: The Analytic Press.

______ & Goldberg, A. (1973). *Models of the Mind.* Chicago: Univ. Chicago Press.

Kohut, H. (1971). *The Analysis of the Self.* New York: Int. Univ. Press.

______ (1984). *How Does Analysis Cure?* Chicago: Univ. Chicago Press.

Moraitis, G. (1988). A reexamination of phobias as the fear of the unknown. *Annual Psychoanal.,* 16:231–249.

Winnicott, D. (1955). Metapsychological and clinical aspects of regression in the psycho-analytical set-up. In *Collected Papers.* New York: Basic Books, 1958, pp. 278–294.

400 E. Randolph Street
Apt. 3724
Chicago, IL 60601

Phobias and the Pursuit of Novelty

GEORGE MORAITIS, M.D.

FREUD'S FORMULATIONS ON PHOBIAS UNDERWENT a continual change that reflects the evolution of psychoanalysis, theoretically and clinically. Despite these changes, however, Freud always maintained, in one form or another, the distinction between phobias as a psychoneurotic symptom and phobias as a symptom of "actual neurosis" the latter carrying the inclusion of a biologically based condition.

For a long time in the clinical situation, the analysis of phobias has been dominated by Freud's (1909) case of Little Hans, in which he conceptualized phobias within the category of a hysterical neurosis. Phobics were identified as the hysterics who are unable to repress their unacceptable wishes and fears and instead displace them onto other objects and situations. The phobic symptom, like the dream, was described as another royal road to the unconscious, the analysis of which one hoped would lead to the uncovering of the unconscious wish and fear of retribution.

In the actual clinical situation, this proved to be a very hard road to travel. Attempts to utilize the psychoanalytic conceptual model in the treatment of phobias have often been ineffective. Freud (1919, pp. 165–166) identified this difficulty when he wrote: "One can hardly master a phobia if one waits till the patient lets the analysis influence him to give it up. He will never in that case bring into the analysis the material indispensable for a convincing

Dr. Moraitis is Training and Supervising Analyst, Chicago Institute for Psychoanalysis; he is on the faculty at Northwestern University.

resolution of phobia." He urged analysts to recommend to their patients to "struggle with their anxiety" in order to achieve "a considerable moderation of the phobia" that would allow them to direct their attention inward and bring into consciousness what had been externalized and denied. One of Freud's explanations for the tenacity with which phobic patients are attached to their symptoms pertained to the intensity of the impulse. He assumed that the analyst's recommendation to his patient to struggle with his anxiety would reinforce the ego's capacity to deal with the anxiety generated by the strong instinctual impulse.

In reviewing the contemporary psychoanalytic literature, we can distinguish two basic directions in conceptualizing phobias. One of these (Lewin, 1952) aims to uncover the unconscious fantasy operating behind the symptom, no matter what the nature of this fantasy may be—oedipal or preoedipal. The other (Wangh, 1959; Kohut, 1984) approaches phobias as a manifestation of a more general and basic pathology, as a result of which the symptom does not become the main focus of the analyst's attention. Instead, the analyst aims to help the patient to better regulate the tension produced by the phobic symptoms so that he can address the fundamental structural deficit upon which all pathology presumably rests.

By and large, the phobic patient who is motivated to remain in analysis for a long time and is capable of doing so will probably experience a gradual lessening of the intensity of the fears, regardless of how his analyst has conceptualized the pathology. With time and patience phobias fade away, but they seldom if ever disappear. By and large the phobic orientation remains and, given certain circumstances, the fear can strike again, and often when not expected.

In a way, phobic patients behave like people with learning disabilities. Facts and reasoning have little effect on their beliefs and fears, and they act as if they have a hidden source of knowledge, on the basis of which they have constructed a highly idiosyncratic and often ridiculous image of external reality, which they systematically reinforce through an elaborate system of avoidances and obsessive-compulsive behavior. Often the phobic patient's strong sense of conviction about the nature of the dreaded external reality parallels the analyst's sense of knowing the content of the patient's unconscious. Under such circumstances, the presumption of knowledge implicit in the attitudes of both analyst and patient obstructs the awareness of their ignorance and erects obstacles to a more open-ended exploration of the phobic symptom.

In a recent publication (Moraitis, 1988) I conceptualized certain kinds of phobias as the fear of the unknown rather than the fear of a wish or danger presumably known on an unconscious level. Instead of assuming that all phobic patients dread the rediscovery of the repressed and displaced, we may in selected cases proceed with the hypothesis that it is the new and the unknown that are feared. For these patients, avoidances do not represent the outcomes of fears, rather, the fears are in the service of avoiding the new and unfamiliar. By avoiding the novel and the unknown they try to maintain a rigid, familiar, and rather limited perception of themselves and the universe within which they experience themselves. The obsessive-compulsive symptomatology commonly observed in these phobic patients represents a restitutional effort, no matter how awkward and logically unattainable, to bring what is novel under the rubric of more archaic perceptual patterns and configurations.

Conceptualizing the phobias as the fear of the unknown is based on the hypothesis that the pursuit of novelty, so clearly evident in infancy, is in essence a basic motivational force in its own right. This assumption resonates with Lichtenberg's (1989) recent formulations about the five basic motivational systems, one of which pertains to the need for exploration.

From birth on, infants seek stimulation by gazing and reaching out for objects around them with curiosity and bewilderment. At first everything must be novel to them, but before long infants learn to distinguish between familiar and unfamiliar stimuli, directing more attention toward the novel and becoming easily bored with the familiar. As the maturational process unfolds, the joyous pursuit of novelty becomes more discriminate and restricted. The infant's stranger anxiety may be an indication of the emerging need to restrict the input of novelty to manageable proportions. Whether the novelty perceived is the absence of mother, the presence of the stranger, or the development of the capacity for fearfulness (Emde, 1976), the fact remains that a threshold has evolved beyond which the strange and the unfamiliar is not tolerated.

We can theorize that the young infant was previously protected from the overwhelming impact of novelty by the immaturity of the nervous system. Lichtenberg (1983) argues persuasively that the infant's response to the stranger constitutes the first example of the functions of the imaging capacity. I believe it is the development of this capacity that becomes the principal regulator of the input of novelty as the child matures.

During the second year of life, the maturing locomotor system gives the pursuit of novelty a more active form. During the rapprochement subphase, toddlers clearly display an intense struggle between the urge to venture into the world that surrounds them and the need to maintain contact with the safe and familiar.

Gradually, however, the development of psychic structure and the establishment of a relatively stable representational world provide the maturing individual with a private universe through which all perceptions are mediated. The presence of this internal universe enables the individual to maintain an idiosyncratic sense of continuity and predictability, on all levels of awareness, through the use of schemas based on past experiences and configurations. Some of these schemas are too rigid to allow for the awareness of novelty and the passing of time; others are more flexible and capable of accommodating a limited input of novelty, provided that it does not exceed a given threshold. Periodically, however, and under the impact of powerful biological and environmental events, a massive input of novelty becomes unavoidable. Under such circumstances, it may not be possible to assimilate such input under existing schemata, and a situation will be created comparable to that of a computer which needs to be reprogrammed to deal with unfamiliar data. Some people are more capable of such reprogramming than others, who may attempt, through a pathological system of avoidances and withdrawals, to reinforce the validity of repetitions based on an obsolete sense of reality.

I postulate that when, in the course of life, situations occur that raise the level of awareness of time and change to such a degree that it cannot be assimilated into the preexisting repetitive schemata, a fundamental change must be instituted, which can be compared to reprogramming. Reprogramming is not simply an adaptive process of incorporating something new into an existing operational mode. It is more than that. When the awareness of novelty becomes the dominant element in one's sense of reality, repetitions assume a defensive function designed to limit the level of such awareness by providing the time for a more gradual internal reorganization of the perceptual schemata that is not simply re-creative, but is to a significant extent original in nature.

We can assume that the capacity for such reorganization has certain biological roots and, to an extent, occurs automatically during certain developmental phases. Epigenetic factors, however, must also be important because they may have fostered or hindered the capacity to "reprogram" during the crucial times in the course of one's development. The understanding of these factors is important because the capacity to reprogram is the ultimate protection against the danger of traumatic overstimulation by the novel, the unfamiliar, and the ambiguous.

Why is such protection needed? Why does novelty constitute a danger to psychological organization? In a sense the answer is biological and pertains to the inherent limitations of our cognitive capabilities to comprehend and master the multiplicity of events, both internal and external, and the rapidity with which they occur. In the psychological realm, the danger is experienced by the sense of mortification generated by the awareness of one's relative insignificance and ignorance when placed within the context of an immense universe and its powerful forces. In contrast, the inner sense of reality creates an illusionary sense of constancy, stability, and predictability within the boundaries of an illusionary but manageable universe that reserves for its creator a central and important position. The need to maintain such constancy must be balanced against the need for exploration and novelty.

Repression and disavowal, defense mechanisms that regulate the need to repeat what on a conscious or unconscious level is familiar but threatening, can protect us from rediscovery but not from the awareness of the new. Protection from the feared unfamiliar and new is achieved through a well-designed system of avoidance characteristic of the person involved. If the unfamiliar stimulus cannot be avoided, a compensatory intensification of reenactments and remembrances will delay the assimilation and accommodation of the novel input.

The effectiveness of such defensive systems will depend to a great extent on the intensity of the thirst for novelty versus the rigidity of the internal representations. I believe that culture and upbringing systematically channel the pursuit of novelty into directions that are relatively safe and predictable. Formal education, religion, and cultural customs and practices are designed to determine not only what the child should learn but also what he should not. The most formidable of the controls, however, are the internal configurations from which there is no escape or avoidance. The romantic notion of turning inward to be liberated from the constraints of an oppressive environment does not take into account the restricting effect of a cyclical and repetitive process that characterizes our inner world.

The encounter with novelty is not always an elective process. The biological changes we must all acknowledge, as well as life events that cannot be avoided, precipitate an input of novelty that must be dealt with regardless of the strength of our motivation to encounter the novel. Freud (1912) referred to novelty when he discussed the taboo of virginity.

The loss of an important object also represents a traumatic encounter with novelty that may threaten the sense of reality as it relates to the sense of self and the surrounding universe. The stability of internal configurations will be undermined and, the first attempt to ward off the input of novelty will be by creating a state of disbelief, a state of ambiguity that provides the necessary time to accommodate the input. Within the context of this discussion, pathological mourning and depression reflect the inability to accommodate the novel input.

In the psychoanalytic literature, the broader pathological manifestations of overstimulation have been identified with the traumatic neuroses, the clinical manifestations of which are well known. Comparable clinical phenomena can be produced by a state of stagnation created by a lack of novel input due to the presence of powerful internal and external barriers. This possibility should be seriously considered when treating patients who seem to deliberately create crises and agitate themselves by provoking the analyst and the environment they live in. Such behaviors have often been mistakenly diagnosed as overstimulation, as a result of which the analyst attempts to pacify the patient through tension-regulation techniques. Such an approach is not likely to produce the desired results inasmuchas pacification is the novel stimulus that the patient is attempting to avoid by creating tensions in the environment and within himself.

The psychopathology pertaining to over- and understimulation by novelty can be conceptualized along the lines of actual neurosis, according to Freud's (1933, pp. 86–88) last definition of the term, that of a basic biological response to threat that lacks symbolic content. Clinically, however, it is always possible to conceptualize some form of symbolic content to all phobic symptoms. When treating patients who experience a basic fear of novelty, interpreting the symbolic content of the fear has little effect on the patient's condition.

Gedo (1979) provides a systematic theoretical and therapeutic reference to deal with such situations that aims to "raise the unrecognized biological goals of the human organism to the level of the person's conscious awareness in order to weave these aims into the self-organization in an optimally adaptive memory" (p. 23). It is my belief that one of those unrecognized aims is the individual's natural thirst for novelty that needs to be raised to the patient's conscious awareness with the help of the analyst in order to make the analysis more relevant and effective.

Kohut's concept of the selfobject (1977, p. 187) is also relevant to this discussion. A need for mirroring and idealization is in a sense an effort to ward off perceptions that are beyond an optimal threshold. Selfobjects are essential in regulating the input of novelty to manageable proportions.

In the treatment of phobias, the analyst is faced with a dilemma. How can he distinguish between phobias produced by displacements, projection, and disavowal and those that have deeper roots?

There are probably no certain ways to make such a distinction during the diagnostic interviews and the early stages of an analysis. By and large, phobias that have penetrated most aspects of the patient's life are not simple displacements, transitory in nature, but represent aspects of a characterological pathology that has deeper roots.

A better distinction, however, between the two kinds of phobia—those produced by the fear of novelty and those caused by displacement, projection, and disavowal—can only be made during the course of the analysis after the transference has been established. Patients with phobias related to the fear of novelty experience outbreaks of phobic anxiety that do not seem to be linked in any persuasive way to the analytic process in general and to the transference in particular. For these patients, such episodes seem to have an existence independent of the analytic process and frustrate the analyst's efforts to predict them or to cause them to dissipate through interpretation.

To illustrate this point, I will provide two fragments from the analyses of two phobic patients.

Ms. A entered analysis at the age of 31 when she became engaged to a wealthy attorney. Soon after their engagement she experienced uncontrollable outbursts of rage toward him, alternating with deep feelings of affection and devotion. Ms. A has three younger brothers. Having been reasonably successful as an artist, she approached marriage with great trepidation, fearing that she would become helplessly dependent, like her self-centered and phobic mother. Her father, a distant and angry man, had shown clear preference for his sons, and undervalued his daughter's accomplishments and capabilities.

The patient approached the analytic sessions with reservations but also with great expectations. The phobic nature of her symptoms became apparent early in the analysis, when it was identified that the episodes of rage were essentially episodes of panic accompanied by a sense of loss of control. As we tried, with the help of a strongly positive and somewhat erotized transference, to explore the origin of these episodes, Ms. A developed an "elevator phobia" that seriously threatened the continuation of the analysis (my office is on the 23rd floor).

Ms. A presented her phobias in dramatic terms, but it was possible to identify the exaggerated sense of helplessness and despair. I interpreted the unconscious meaning of her symptoms in the context of the transference. More specifically, I referred to her urge to flee in order to avoid the recognition of her transference feelings and expectations. I invited her to "struggle with her fears" so that the analysis could proceed, and after a period of ambivalence and uncertainty it became apparent that she was winning the battle. She overcame the elevator phobia, which did not reappear until the end of the analysis, four years later, when she was preparing herself to tell me "good-bye" as a happily married woman.

It appeared that Ms. A's phobia was primarily the result of strong erotic and hostile feelings that originated in her early experiences with her father and had been displaced onto her husband and the analyst. The phobias appeared under certain circumstances when she felt under pressure to enter into intimate relationships with men and to deal with her ambivalence about them and her identification with her phobic mother. After those issues were addressed in the analysis, the phobic symptoms subsided, suggesting that the diagnostic formulations made had been validated clinically.

In this case too, however, I could identify issues pertaining to the encounter with novelty. Her engagement to get married and the beginning of the analysis constituted powerful novel input that aroused fears and apprehension. Her urge to explore and discover, however, was stronger than her fears and inhibitions. It can be argued that what I describe as the urge to explore is another way of referring to her aggression and need to control and dominate. Essentially, in this case the issue is a matter of definition of what constitutes aggression and how this relates to the pursuit of novelty. With Ms. A, the question was academic. In the next clinical illustration, also discussed in my 1988 paper, the situation was different.

Mrs. B's analysis began when she was 35 years old. Married, the mother of three, her phobias began approximately three or four years earlier, and were precipitated by a cervical biopsy. Although the results of the biopsy were negative and the patient properly reassured, she developed intense fears of cancer and instituted an elaborate system of avoidances of people and situations designed to prevent her being contaminated with "cancerous materials." The subsequent development of obsessive-compulsive symptoms gradually made her a virtual prisoner in her own house.

Mrs. B is a very creative good-looking woman, intense and highly energetic. She was born and raised in this country, but her parents came to the United States as refugees from Europe in the early twenties, having been the victims of political persecution. She was raised in a strict Christian environment in which her parents' code of behavior and set of values were presented in no uncertain terms. Although the patient reported some mild fears in childhood, there is no history of phobias prior to the onset of her present illness.

Mrs. B's mother consistently identified the patient as "lucky." That conveyed to the patient a sense of envy and competition.

At the time the phobias appeared, the patient's husband had achieved some important successes in business, and the family became very secure financially. It was at the same time, however, that her father died after a long illness.

It was easy to identify the fear of death in the patient's phobic preoccupations. I linked the illness and death of her father to her fears about cancer, a fact that led me to believe that Mrs. B was in a state of pathological mourning reaction. The patient, who quickly sensed from my questions the line of my thinking, had no difficulty with this formulation. The presence of an idealizing and somewhat erotized transference provided some further indication of the patient's effort to replace the lost object and lessen the frightening identification with her deceased father.

As the process unfolded, however, I was impressed with the fact of how well things were progressing in the analytic situation and how little difference this seemed to make as far as the phobic symptoms were concerned. When I brought this to the attention of the patient, it produced a somewhat explosive response. She felt she had displeased me. She became frightened and apologetic. She made a deliberate effort to overcome her fears and engage in some activities she had difficulty with, but despite some minor successes, by and large the fears remained. I thought the time was ripe to address the issue of her desire to please, an issue that helped us focus primarily on her relationship with her mother. She recalled with pain some agonizing efforts to please her mother and her consistent failure in doing so.

During that period of time my patient became increasingly more curious about my background, asking me to provide her with information about historical events she assumed I was familiar with, and which her mother had directly experienced. Such questions she had never asked her mother or, if she did, she never felt she received satisfactory answers to. In analyzing her curiosity, once more I had the feeling of a very meaningful and intense analytic process in the clinical situation, but the question remained, how did this really affect the phobias, the symptoms that originally brought her into analysis? It was quite evident that gradually the patient's episodes of panic diminished; she was less anxious in the clinical situation and capable of performing her daily activities at home. Although her fears were reduced, her avoidance of places, situations, and people who could activate these fears remained strong. The patient became able to better master the anxiety, should anxiety erupt, but both of us were keenly aware of the potential for a new outbreak of fear, and of the fact that her basic phobic orientation to life had remained the same. At that time I considered of particular importance the fact that these outbreaks of fear, whether intense or mild, did not seem to be linked in any apparent way to the analytic process in general or to the transference in particular. Consistently, the patient's phobic responses were mobilized when she was confronted with a situation that required she take some action in a direction she was unfamiliar with. It did not seem that such incidents represented the acting out of a conflict mobilized in the clinical situation. Yet the oedipal and narcissistic issues were clear and evident both in the transference and in the patient's history as presented, and our analytic work was effective insofar as these issues were concerned. The erotic attachment to her father, the issues of envy and competition with her mother and brother, as well as her archaic needs for a holding environment were properly recognized and addressed. None of these issues, however, generated the intensity of the affects of the phobic reaction, the abrupt outburst of which would overshadow everything else. These episodes seemed to have, to an extent at least, an independent existence.

It is hard to overestimate the frustrating effect such phenomena have upon the patient and the analyst, and how easily they can facilitate a sense of therapeutic pessimism.

The therapeutic impasse encountered in the analysis of some phobias constitutes a scientific anomaly that threatens the paradigm of psychoanalysis. Elsewhere (Moraitis, 1981) I have described the analytic response to such anomalies and the need to recognize and report clinical data that cannot be explained with the existing psychoanalytic models, or data which seem to contradict them. As the psychoanalytic clinician distinguishes between what is more or less known and understandable and what is neither known nor understandable, he gradually defines areas of ignorance, the recognition of which is essential for the successful outcome of all analyses, and in the analysis of phobias in particular.

The analysis of the transference and the search for the unconscious meaning of the patient's communication represent fundamental aspects of the analytic enterprise. Neither of these objectives, however, can be carried out successfully without the appreciation of the inherent limitations in understanding the complexities involved and the capacity to tolerate ambiguity and ignorance. Consistently the fear of the unknown leads to unwarranted presumption of knowledge. To counteract the phobic patient's preposterous presumption of knowledge, the analyst must utilize his own capacity to tolerate ambiguity and admit ignorance.

In my analytic work with Mrs. B, I was impressed by the restrictive nature of the universe upon which her perceptions rest, and the dread with which she approached any possibility of expanding its boundaries. I hypothesized that the archaic model upon which Mrs. B's perceptions were organized was designed to systematically discourage curiosity and search, and avoid states of doubt and bewilderment. Accordingly, trial-and-error experiences were limited, while circular, repetitive patterns of behavior were reinforced.

The psychological organization of Mrs. B can be compared to a totalitarian state which, in order to maintain the consistency of its rigid organization, must avoid threatening novelty and the affective response it generates. If avoidance is impossible, a state of emergency will be created, a state of panic, which will block the input of any further stimulus by the powerful affects mobilized. Panic represents the brutal force that will obliterate all perceptions and give priority to only one, the phobia, which thus becomes the instrument through which an obsolete model of the world and of the self will be maintained.

The metaphor I used is designed to illustrate both the intensity with which this phobic patient experienced her condition as externally imposed, as well as the possibility that the patient's perception of danger is not necessarily illusionary in nature. The danger may not be reminiscences repressed or displaced, but alient perceptual input that threatens the patient's psychological organization due to her limited capacity to cope with ambiguity and ignorance.

Mrs. B experienced her phobic symptom as a programmed response to repeat thoughts and actions despite her strong sense of conviction that she "ought to know better." Repetitions in life and in the analytic situation are of course always observed and associated with transferences. There is, however, a substantial difference in the versatility and variability with which these repetitions appear and are experienced. Hypothetically, we can place on one end of the spectrum repetitions with greater versatility and variability. Such repetitions may be difficult to recognize, for both analyst and analysand, without the use of symbolism and imagination, because the repetitive elements involved are intertwined with several novel elements each time they appear. At the other end of the spectrum we can place repetitions with little versatility and variability which are probably close to what Freud referred to as repetition compulsion. Phobic responses constitute the compulsive repetition of affective states and avoidances that does not allow for any novel elements to enter into it. They can better be compared to repetition compulsions than to transference reactions. The phobic patient's persistent perception of the symptom in concrete and external terms frustrates the analyst's effort to influence it through a systematic search of its meaning. When this occurs, both patient and analyst assume the presence of a master who dominates the patient's life experiences, whom neither can control.

In reviewing Mrs. B's history, it is relatively easy to identify the masters who systematically programmed her early experiences. Being the daughter of two frightened and severely traumatized refugees, she was raised in an atmosphere of suspicion, superstition, and relative isolation. A set of unnegotiable and unexplained prohibitions were imposed upon her since early childhood. Paradoxically, the patient did not resent these prohibitions and did not object to them. It gradually became evident that she did not perceive her parents' attitudes and prohibitions as the reflection of their own narcissistic need to intimidate and control. Instead, she perceived their behavior as the outgrowth of their true conviction of the actual nature of the reality they lived in, and their sense of parental responsibility to protect and guide. Under the circumstances, it would have been impossible for her to doubt the question her parents' perceptions, which by all indications were based on their actual experiences. With ingenuity and hard work she managed for a long time to avoid a direct confrontation between the small world upon which her perceptions were organized and the larger world she was operating in. She went through the developmental period of adolescence and young childhood with little discomfort. But gradually she became increasingly phobic in her middle thirties, several years after her marriage and the birth of her children. At the time the phobic symptoms appeared she had distanced herself from the family of origin. The death of her father, the illness and professional success of her husband, the increasing affluence of the family, and the involvement in a larger social and family milieu, had created for her a world both different and apart from the one she was raised in. Overwhelmed by the novelty of it all, she approached psychoanalytic treatment in the hope of finding a new programmer who would dictate the new program that would enable her to deal with the new realities.

In clinical psychoanalysis, the encounter with novelty is not limited to the patient. The analyst, too, is encountering novelty as he attempts to organize the phobic patient's subjective experiences into coherent schemas. However, the more he resists the temptation of premature closure, the freer he will be to consider alternative ways to understand the observations made. It is important for the analyst to appreciate the patient's efforts to create a new sense of reality, a new synthesis that is original in nature. In order to facilitate the patient's capacity to deal with novelty, the analyst must have some thirst for novelty too.

All phobic patients come to analysis hoping to be rescued from a vicious circular process of behavior and thinking that has obstructed the input of novelty and created a sense of emptiness and stagnation. Such an obstruction may be primary, as with Mrs. B, or defensive in nature, as with Ms. A. Seeking analysis, however, is in itself a pursuit of novelty and is therefore dreaded and feared as much as it is desired, and approached with great expectations.

The rather dramatic effects the beginning of therapy has for many patients has often been conceptualized as a transference cure and interpreted as the outgrowth of a repetition linked to the memory of a caretaker lending a helpful hand in a moment of distress. I believe that in some patients such phenomena can better be explained as a result of the novel input generated by initiating the therapeutic enterprise. After a while the novelty wears off, and often it does not take too long for the therapeutic sessions to become part of a routine, a ritual, which sooner or later is going to replace the sense of novelty the first encounters aroused.

If successful, however, the analytic process that is set in motion will produce other sources of novel input. One such source pertains to the patient's emerging capacity to listen to himself. Free associating requires a slowing-down in the mode of the thinking process, which brings into awareness novel connections and meanings. To facilitate such a development, the analyst assists his patient in maintaining the proper level of curiosity, intellectual honesty, and tolerance of ambiguity.

To open up the closed psychological system within each the phobic patient has incarcerated himself or herself, an attitude must prevail that discourages premature closures and excessive eagerness to arrive at the answers. It is tolerance of ambiguity and ignorance that must be cultivated rather than the arrival at the correct answers.

In the analysis of phobias more than in other analyses it is essential that the analyst maintain a sense of unpredictability in his responses by avoiding redundant observations and interpretations. The analytic process should be flexible enough to generate different lines of interpretation and to recognize the interpretive errors of both of the participants involved. I would like to clarify that I am not advocating a deliberate evasiveness and an attitude that conveys from both sides an absence of a sense of conviction and discovery. Such an attitude would turn the analytic process into a meaningless intellectual exercise. What I refer to is the need to avoid situations in which the therapeutic process has come to halt through the inability of both patient and analyst to avoid a cyclical repetitive pattern that provides diminishing returns.

The stories our phobic patients tell us are in many ways preposterous. They are the by-products of a basic constraint under the influence of which the patient's thinking operates. Such constraints, on the one hand, limit the choice of the patient's communications, and on the other, facilitate the structure and direction of his associations and behavior. They represent the demons or the angels of his past that he is programmed to obey. As we listen carefully we come to realize the degree to which the phobic patients struggle to escale the scenario created by them or imposed upon them, and to rewrite that story in a somewhat unique and original way. If the analyst becomes too preoccupied with assimilating his patient's story with his own theoretical schemata he may very well fail to appreciate his patient's need to write the story anew.

It is my belief that the phobic system does not necessarily represent a point of fixation, a reactivation of the past for the past's sake. In some cases the problem lies in the absence of the necessary schemata that would enable the individual to assimilate and accommodate the novel input. The repetitions in the transference phenomena observed are compensatory in nature and aim to substitute for the missing tools while avoiding the novel input. Depending on the level of the intensity of the regressive pull the patient is experiencing, those transferences may reflect the reactivation of partially repressed configurations or take the form of more archaic phenomena that can be described as repetition compulsion devoid of symbolic content. In a therapeutic sense, tracing the origin of these repetitions can only be of limited value to these patients because it does not address the basic pathology involved, which pertains to their incapacity to assimilate the new with the old.

What I describe can be identified as a deficit that has its roots in the early stages of an individual's development. I use the term *deficit,* however, without implying a primitive psychological organization. Experience has taught me that an individual's limitations in accommodating novel input is by no means limited to people with primitive character structures. Often the construction of a new sense of reality may be considerably more difficult with some of the more psychologically well-organized individuals than with some of the more primitive ones. The phobic patients I refer to are not primitive individuals when their overall psychological organization is taken into account. Their psychopathology is circumscribed and does not become evident until such time as the registration of an overwhelming sense of novelty becomes unavoidable.

In the analytic situation, phobic patients often come across as psychologically unsophisticated and as needing to "externalize" the nature of their symptom. They also seem controlling and demanding, with tendencies to make the analytic treatment a ritualistic process devoid of uncertainties and novelty. In many ways they behave like patients in a post-traumatic state who need comfort and reassurance.

The holding environment of the psychoanalytic situation will provide for some of the patients' needs, as they pertain to the state of shock that they may be in. Through the analyst's interpretations and their own introspective efforts, phobic patients come gradually to the realization of the restricting effect of the transference repetitions upon their personality and creativity. As useful as such enlightenment may be, it is very difficult for phobic patients to transform restricting and rigid perceptual schemata into more flexible structures that can accommodate novel input. Theoretically speaking, the so-called "resolution of the transference" implies that the conscious awareness of the meaning of transference repetitions should enable the patient to move beyond such repetitions and reenactments. But what lies beyond? Freud wrote (1919, p. 161) that "The psycho-synthesis is . . . achieved during analytic treatment without our intervention, automatically and inevitably." Psychosynthesis does not seem to be automatic or inevitable with some phobic patients. On the contrary, those I refer to seem to need more than the insights gained in the analytic situation. They must broaden the boundaries of their self-inquiry beyond the protective analytic situation by becoming involved in some original enterprise, the nature and direction of which only the patient can determine. They must take some action in a novel direction.

The enterprise the patient may choose could be a new relationship, a new professional activity, a new artistic product or business venture. It may be an enterprise, ambitious or humble, to which the patient dedicates a good deal of creativity, not as an escape from the analytic situation but as a creative extension of it designed to practice what he or she learned and test the validity of the insights outside the analytic context. This testing reveals the relative accuracy and limitations of the insights gained. No interpretation or explanation can stand the test of time for very long without being qualified or discarded. Naturally, such discovery would produce disappointment, but also excitement. Discovering the limitations of the analyst's knowledge is a fundamental growth experience for the analysand. The patient's awareness of the analyst's limitations is the indication of his growing knowledge, which also facilitates the patient's tolerance of his own limitations in due time.

By and large, phobics, must more than other analytic patients, are very reluctant to take the analyst's interpretations and explanations at face value. Having been traumatized by the blind convictions and beliefs of their caretakers, they experience an overwhelming sense of doubt about the reliability of all authorities. Often the analyst's interpretations come across to the phobic patient as preposterous as the patient's phobic preoccupations come across to the analyst. To achieve a level of effective communication they both must gradually come to terms with their unwarranted presumptions of knowledge. Instead of the compelling search for the ultimate answers, it is the multiplicity of the variables involved that should be addressed in order to maintain an ongoing process of creating a new sense of reality.

Theoretical considerations about the pursuit of novelty constitute in their essence an aspect of motivational theory that aims to study man's need to explore and discover. Many psychoanalysts have been reluctant to expand the motivational theory in psychoanalysis. The increased awareness of the complexities in the clinical situation has made such expansion inevitable. I offered the above conceptualizations in the belief that certain kinds of phobias must be reexamined under the light of a broader motivational theory that takes into account man's thirst for novelty along with that for pleasure.

REFERENCES

Emde, R. (1976). *Emotional Expression in Infancy. Psycholog. Issues, Monogr.* 37. New York: Int. Univ. Press.

Freud, S. (1909). Analysis of a phobia in a 5 year old boy. *S.E.,* 10.

_____ (1912). Contribution to the psychology of love. *S.E.,* 11.

_____ (1919). Lines of advance in psycho-analytic therapy. *S.E.,* 17.

_____ (1933). New introductory lectures in psychoanalysis. *S.E.,* 22.

Gedo, J. (1979). *Beyond Interpretation.* New York: Int. Univ. Press.

Kohut, H. (1977). *The Restoration of the Self.* New York: Int. Univ. Press.

_____ (1984), *How Does Analysis Cure?* Chicago: Univ. Chicago Press.

Lewin, B. (1952). Phobic symptoms and dream interpretation. *Psychoanal. Q.,* 21:295–322.

Lichtenberg, J. (1983). *Psychoanalysis and Infant Research.* Hillsdale, NJ: The Analytic Press.

_____ (1989). *Psychoanalysis and Motivation.* Hillsdale, NJ: The Analytic Press.

Moraitis, G. (1981). The analyst's response to the limitations of his science. *Psychoanal. Inquiry,* 2:57–79.

_____ (1988). A reexamination of phobias as the fear of the unknown. *Annual Psychoanal.,* 16. New York: Int. Univ. Press.

Waugh, M. (1959). The structural determinants of phobia. *J. Amer. Psychoanal. Assn.,* 7:675–694.

180 North Michigan Avenue
Chicago, IL 60601

Neurophysiological, Cognitive-Behavioral, and Psychoanalytic Approaches to Panic Disorder: Toward an Integration

FREDRIC N. BUSCH, M.D.,
ARNOLD M. COOPER, M.D.
GERALD L. KLERMAN, M.D.,
ROBERT J. PENZER, M.D.,
THEODORE SHAPIRO, M.D., and
M. KATHERINE SHEAR, M.D.

IN HIS EARLY WORK FREUD (1895b) made a clear distinction between anxiety neurosis, which he described in terms that closely parallel the current DSM IIIR definition of panic disorder, and psychoneurotic states. He viewed anxiety neurosis, along with neurasthenia, as "actual neuroses" with a somatic etiology, requiring a nonpsychological treatment (a change in sexual behavior). Psychoneuroses (phobia, obsessive compulsive disorder, hysteria), in which anxiety was psychically bound, arose from

Dr. Busch is Instructor in Psychiatry, Cornell University Medical College.
Dr. Cooper is Professor of Psychiatry, Cornell University Medical College.
Dr. Klerman is Associate Chairman for Research and Professor of Psychiatry, Cornell University Medical College.
Dr. Penzer is Senior Clinical Associate in Psychiatry, Cornell University Medical College.
Dr. Shapiro is Professor of Psychiatry and Professor of Psychiatry in Pediatrics, Cornell University Medical College.
Dr. Shear is Associate Professor of Clinical Psychiatry, Cornell University Medical College.

psychic conflict caused by early developmental traumas and therefore was accessible to a psychoanalytic treatment. Freud never fully abandoned his view of actual neuroses, referring in "Inhibitions, Symptoms and Anxiety" (1926) to one type of anxiety that "was involuntary, automatic and always justified on economic grounds" (p. 162). In this work, however, Freud revised his theory of anxiety, describing it as an intrapsychic response to psychologically meaningful dangers. In addition to automatic anxiety, he described a second type of anxiety that signaled the ego to institute defense against the danger of emergent forbidden wishes. The new theory of anxiety as a response to danger led Freud to delineate a series of developmentally significant fears: helplessness, separation, castration, and finally, in its most mature form, superego anxiety. Many psychoanalysts, using the new theory, came to view any form of anxiety as secondary to the emergence of forbidden unconscious wishes, requiring a psychoanalytic approach. This view, however, ignored Freud's proviso that under certain conditions, such as acute trauma, automatic anxiety could break through and be expressed as panic.

In recent years interest in psychoanalytic theories and treatments of panic disorder has been overshadowed by the advent of neurophysiological and cognitive-behavioral approaches. Psychopharmacologists have returned to a view of panic disorder as a different form of anxiety with a neurophysiological basis, responsive to psychotropic medications. Cognitive-behavioral theorists, while accepting a psychological etiology of panic, focus on catastrophic misinterpretation of somatic sensations rather than intrapsychic conflict. Whereas little systematic research has been done on psychoanalytic treatments of panic, pharmacological and cognitive-behavioral treatments have been systematically studied and demonstrated to provide rapid and effective relief of panic symptoms in many patients.

However, neurophysiological and cognitive-behavioral theories and treatments of panic leave some unresolved questions and treatment problems that may be answered by the psychoanalytic approach. The neurophysiological and cognitive-behavioral theories do not explain associated maladaptive traits in these patients that appear to precede the onset of panic disorder, nor do they fully explain the timing of the onset of panic disorder. Moreover, some patients are unable to tolerate or do not respond to either pharmacological or cognitive-behavioral treatments. Additionally, relapse rates after these treatments have not been adequately studied, but may be substantial. Finally, pharmacological and cognitive-behavioral treatments focus on the symptoms of panic disorder, and it is unclear whether these treatments address significant related psychosocial difficulties of these patients. A study by Markowitz et al. (1989) found that panic disorder was associated with significant impairment in social and occupational functioning, as well as increased alcohol and drug abuse and financial dependency. Integrating the psychoanalytic approach with the neurophysiologic and cognitive-behavioral approaches may lead to a broader understanding of panic vulnerability and a more complete treatment of panic disorder and its associated psychosocial morbidity.

To explore these issues, we first examine in more detail the assets, liabilities, and implications of the neurophysiological and cognitive-behavioral approaches to panic. We then present a formulation that integrates social interaction, intrapsychic functioning, and neurophysiology. We conclude by addressing issues of appropriate treatment interventions and directions for future research.

Neurophysiological and Cognitive-Behavioral Approaches

Several lines of evidence support a neurophysiological basis for panic disorder, including twin and family studies, measurements of baseline autonomic activity, studies of pharmacological provocation of panic, and studies of brain neurochemistry. The information presented here is in part drawn from reviews by Gorman et al. (1989) and Shear and Fyer (1988). Torgerson (1983) studied rates of anxiety disorders in monozygotic (MZ) and dizygotic (DZ) twins. He found that 31 percent of MZ twins were concordant for anxiety disorder with panic attacks compared to 0 percent of DZ twins, a significant difference. Crowe et al. (1983) found significantly higher rates of panic disorder in families of panic patients compared to families of control groups. These studies provide strong evidence of a genetic basis for panic disorder. The findings, however, do not necessarily support a neurophysiological etiology of panic, for psychological processes may also be genetically transmitted.

Baseline measurements in panic patients generally reveal elevated heart rate, skin conductance, and blood pressure, correlating with increased anxiety or fearfulness. A study by Shear et al. (1987) found a higher-than-normal mean daily density of ventricular premature complexes in panic patients. Thus panic patients may have an autonomic dysfunction secondary to a neurophysiological vulnerability. Provocation of panic via pharmacological agents has been widely used to investigate pathogenic mechanisms in panic. Sodium lactate infusion has been found to induce panic in most patients with panic disorder. Other agents found consistently to cause panic in vulnerable individuals include yohimbine, caffeine, and inhalation of 5 percent CO_2. Multiple studies have led to the hypothesis that an abnormality in central noradrenergic functioning can lead to panic attacks. Provocation of panic by yohimbine supports this theory, because yohimbine activates the noradrenergic system through blockade of a receptor that inhibits noradrenergic release. The likely site of the abnormality is the locus ceruleus, which contains many noradrenergic cell bodies. A study of the stump-tailed monkey found that electrical stimulation of the locus ceruleus leads to a panic-like state. Tricyclic antidepressants, which effectively block panic attacks, have been found to decrease the locus ceruleus firing rate.

Other studies indicate that the neurophysiological abnormalities in panic disorder involve more than shifts in noradrenergic functioning. Lactate and CO_2 induction of panic, for example, may involve stimulation of medullary chemoreceptors. Some studies suggest that the serotonergic system, including the midbrain dorsal raphe, may also play a role in panic onset. These data have led Gorman et al. (1989) to propose a hypothesis that panic results from an inherited hyperexcitability in one or more of three brainstem areas: the locus ceruleus, the medullary chemoreceptors, and the midbrain dorsal raphe.

The neurophysiological approach to panic disorder has led to rapid alleviation of panic symptoms in many patients through psychopharmacological intervention. Treatment centers on medications that purport to reverse the neurophysiological abnormalities in these patients. As noted above, tricyclic antidepressants (and MAO inhibitors), which affect the noradrenergic system, have been found to be effective. The antidepressants fluoxitene and clomipramine, which affect the serotonergic system, also block panic. Additionally, alprazolam, a benzodiazepine, can effectively treat panic symptoms, although the mechanism of action remains unclear.

One problem with the neurophysiological theory is the difficulty in explaining what triggers the expression of the neurophysiological abnormality that leads to panic onset. Here psychosocial factors, which are not focused on in neurophysiologic theory, may play a role. Many studies indicate that significant life events precede the onset of panic disorder (Solyom et al., 1974; Last et al., 1984; Faravelli, 1985; Roy-Byrne et al., 1986). Life events have been defined in various ways, but according to Dohrenwend et al. (1978): "The common denominator in these definitions is objective occurrences of sufficient magnitude to bring about change in the usual activities of most individuals who experience them" (p. 207). Life events strain adaptive coping mechanisms. Life events found to precede panic onset usually involve a loss or rejection, an increase in expectations that requires more independent behavior, or a change in job or location. Recently, two studies used more systematic approaches with control groups to examine life events in panic disorder. Faravelli (1985) found a higher number of life events in panic patients compared to healthy controls in the 12 months preceding the onset of panic. The author noted that "both loss events and threatening events seem to play a role" (p. 105) in panic onset. Roy-Byrne et al. (1986) found that panic patients reported significantly more life events that happened to them personally in the 12 months preceding panic compared to controls. The patients also described significantly more subjective distress about their events compared to controls; events were viewed as more undesirable, uncontrollable, and caused extreme lowering of self-esteem.

These stressors may trigger the expression of a neurophysiological abnormality. However, the mechanism by which an external event can lead to the expression of this abnormality is not understood. Additionally, since each individual interprets the meaning of these events differently, an external stressor may or may not lead to the onset of panic in a neurophysiologically susceptible individual. This suggests that there is a crucial psychological variable that mediates between external events and panic onset.

The cognitive-behavioral or learning theory posits one means by which interpretation of sensory data may lead to the onset of panic. According to this model, as reviewed by Craske (1988), catastrophic misinterpretation of somatic sensations (referred to as interoceptive cues) occurs, leading to a feeling of imminent danger. For example, mild, normal chest pain may be inaccurately interpreted as a heart attack. The patients may also exaggerate the danger of external events. Once a panic episode has occurred, further panic attacks may be triggered in response to associated cues by a classical conditioning mechanism. Agoraphobia can develop secondary to avoidance of situations in which these cues are present. Freud (1895a) appears to have had a similar idea when he reported: "In the case of agoraphobia, etc., we often find *the recollection of an anxiety attack;* and what the patient actually fears is the occurrence of such an attack under the special conditions in which he believes he cannot escape it" (p. 81).

Cognitive-behavioral treatment focuses on correcting catastrophic misinterpretation through cognitive and behavioral techniques. The cognitive approach involves providing information that leads to a more accurate appraisal of the danger of interoceptive cues or external events. In interoceptive exposure, the central behavioral approach, panic patients are exposed repeatedly to interoceptive cues, which are induced by a variety of techniques, e.g., hyperventilation. Over time the patient gains a sense of control over and familiarity with these cues rather than a sense of danger. The success of cognitive-behavioral treatments indicates that a focus on psychological functioning alone can affect a disorder that may have a neurophysiological basis. The cognitive-behavioral approach also demonstrates that a neurophysiological predisposition alone cannot fully account for panic vulnerability and that a psychological factor, catastrophic misinterpretation, must also be included. A study by Shear et al. (in press) found that lactate induction of panic can be reversed after successful cognitive treatment of panic; i.e., a psychological intervention altered neurophysiological function.

The cognitive-behavioral theory, however, also does not fully address the issues of panic vulnerability. Although cognitive-behavioral theory describes catastrophic misinterpretation of life events, the reason that a particular life event is so misinterpreted and how it triggers panic is not fully explained. The meaning of the event to that individual, as well as other affects triggered by that event, may play a role. Additionally, the basis of a tendency to misinterpret catastrophically is not explained. Individuals with different personality organizations may vary in their tendency to misinterpret catastrophically somatic sensations or external events. Particular premorbid maladaptive traits may predispose to catastrophic misinterpretation. Although not systematically studied, observers from multiple theoretical perspectives have viewed panic patients as pervasively unassertive, fearful, and dependent prior to the onset of panic disorder, thereby undercutting the notion that these symptoms are the results of the panic attack. Marks (1970), for example, reported that the majority of agoraphobics had a premorbid personality "variously described as 'soft', passive, anxious, shy and dependent" (p. 541). Klein (1964) found that half of his patients were "fearful and dependent children, with marked separation anxiety, and difficulty in adjusting to school" (p. 405). He stated that this group "seems to have suffered from a chronically high separation anxiety level throughout life and to have developed panic attacks under conditions where they were peculiarly vulnerable" (pp. 405–406). Torgerson (1986) found a significantly higher rate of reported chronic anxiety in childhood in a panic disorder group compared to a group of patients with generalized anxiety disorder. Unassertiveness may be accompanied by difficulty tolerating anger in patients with panic disorder. Deutsch (1929) described how anxiety is reduced in the presence of a phobic companion because the patient is unconsciously relieved that his aggressive impulses have not harmed this person. Korn et al. (1990) recently described four cases in which anger or frustration were felt to be precipitants of panic attacks. The authors reviewed four prior cases in the literature in which angry affects or aggressive behavior preceded or accompanied panic attacks.

Recent studies by Kagan and colleagues (Rosenbaum et al., 1988; Biederman et al., 1990, Kagan et al., 1990) suggest that individuals at risk for panic disorder (specifically, offspring of parents with panic disorder and agoraphobia) demonstrate a high rate of behavioral inhibition and autonomic arousal in unfamiliar situations very early in life. Biederman et al. (1990) also reported that the inhibited infants and children "manifested long latencies to interact when exposed to novelty, retreated from the unfamiliar, and ceased play and vocalizations while clinging to their mothers" (p. 21). The behavioral inhibition in unfamiliar situations has been demonstrated to be maintained in most cases through infancy, toddlerhood, and school age. In addition, behavioral inhibition has been found to be correlated with increased risk of multiple anxiety, overanxious, and phobic disorders in these children. Although these findings may be viewed as evidence of biologically preprogrammed temperaments in patients predisposed to panic disorder, the temperament described here may also lead to particular forms of psychological disturbances, such as fear of separation, that may increase the risk of panic onset. We discuss below the interaction of temperament and psychological vulnerability to panic in greater detail.

Another psychological phenomenon not well explained by cognitive-behavioral or neurophysiological theories that may also predispose to panic is the presence of particular perceptions of parents found in panic patients. Multiple observers have found that panic patients have internal representations of their parents as, variously, overprotective, restricting, controlling, critical, frightening, and rejecting. For example, Tucker (1956), in a study of 100 phobic patients without a control group, described reports of a "lack of parental affection, overprotection and overcriticism by parents . . ." (p. 827) in 77 of the cases. More recently, further confirmation of these observations has come from more systematic studies that assess parental perceptions with questionnaires that have been found to be highly reliable and valid. Parker (1979), using the Parental Bonding Instrument, found that a group of social phobics and agoraphobics viewed their parents as significantly less caring and more overprotective than controls. This was later confirmed by Silove (1986) for a group of agoraphobics compared to a control group. Arrindell et al. (1983), using a more detailed questionnaire, the Egna Minnen Betraffande Uppfostran (EMBU), found that agoraphobics viewed both parents as having significantly less emotional warmth and mothers as being more rejecting than controls.

A pilot study done at Payne Whitney Clinic adds data that support the relevance of predisposing psychological factors and meaningful life events to panic onset. Pretreatment psychodynamic interviews of nine consecutive patients who met criteria for panic disorder were conducted by trained analysts (A.M.C. and T.S.). Videotapes of these interviews were reviewed by a research psychiatrist (F.N.B.) and rated as to stressors preceding panic, tolerance of anger, sexual conflicts, perceptions of parents, and maladaptive behaviors and attitudes other than panic. Contrary to the currently common assumption that panic attacks emerge "out of the blue," identifiable apparently meaningful stressors preceded the onset of panic in each case. All of the events entailed a loss or an increase in expectations of the patients. Loss events included separations, either emotional or physical, from a significant person in the patient's life. Increases in expectations included increased responsibilities in work or school. The interviews often revealed that the events had particular meanings for patients related to their perception of childhood experiences and often represented a threat to attachment. Seven of nine patients reported difficulty managing angry feelings. Sexual conflicts were not prominent in panic onset and, when present, appeared to be secondary to fears about insecure attachment and angry feelings. The patients variously described their parents as critical, frightening, fearful, hot-tempered, overbearing, competitive, demanding, and judgmental. Each patient described significant interpersonal difficulties, and seven of nine had some identified occupational dysfunction. In evaluating the stressors preceding panic in these patients, it was unclear whether these stressors were of major etiologic significance in triggering panic or whether the stressors were given increased significance after the panic in order to rationalize its onset. In either case, the external world is highly relevant to panic, whether as a precipitant or as an external psychological explanation. A prospective study of the impact of life events could better clarify this issue.

Despite the important successes, then, with neurophysiological and cognitive-behavioral approaches, significant psychological data have not been explained with these theories. Furthermore, there are a number of case reports of successful treatment of panic disorder through psychoanalysis or psychodynamic psychotherapy (Sifneos, 1972; Malan, 1979; Mann & Goldman, 1982; Sandler, 1988; Abend, 1989; Silber, 1989; Milrod & Shear, in press). These reports suggest that dynamic mechanisms may alone account for symptoms and that this alternative treatment can bring relief, sometimes as rapidly as medication or cognitive-behavioral therapy. While these studies are not systematic, they cannot be dismissed in constructing an etiologic theory of panic disorder. In the following section we use these data to develop an integrated formulation that includes neurophysiological and cognitive-behavioral concepts, but also constructs a more comprehensive explanation for panic vulnerability, onset, and premorbid personality disturbances.

An Integrated Approach to Panic Disorder

The formulation we describe postulates a neurophysiological and psychological vulnerability to panic, stemming from a particular constitutional predisposition and/or a specific set of early life experiences. A starting point for our formulation is the observation by Kagan and colleagues (1990) that children of panic disorder patients, presumed to be at risk for the development of panic disorder, show evidence of striking behavioral inhibition and heightened physiological arousal in an experimental situation testing reactions to novelty. The findings are interpreted as evidence of an inborn excessive fearfulness of unfamiliar situations, or shyness. We believe that this temperament will broadly affect the psychological functioning of these children, placing them at increased risk for panic disorder. We suggest that an excessive fearfulness of the unfamiliar will lead the child to develop feelings of heightened dependency on the parent, or on the familiar parent surrogate, to maintain a sense of safety and to modulate intense affects. In an attempt to avoid anxiety, the child develops the wish that the parent be present at all times for protection. Since even in the best of circumstances, a parent cannot always be available for this purpose, the child develops a sense of fearful dependency on this parent who is perceived as "unreliable." As Bowlby (1973) stated, the child will have "no confidence that his attachment figures will be accessible and responsive to him when he wants them to be" (p. 213). This fearful dependency can become a source of narcissistic humiliation for the child, as the failure of the parent to be available at his will elicits feelings of helplessness and demonstrates to him his own incapacity for handling the unfamiliar. In an attempt to alleviate this painful, narcissistic humiliation, the fearful dependency is blamed on the parent, who is fantasied as the source of anxiety via excessive abandoning, frightening or guilt-provoking behaviors. The child will then internalize a representation of the parent as unstable, rejecting and controlling.

This fearful dependency may be derived from the interaction of a fearful constitutional predisposition with ordinary failures of parental care (as we described in Kagan's "shy" children) or from the effect of a particular group of traumatic developmental experiences on an unremarkable predisposition. As Bowlby (1973) demonstrated, the vicissitudes of childhood may include separations or threats of separation that seem insignificant to the parent but may be highly traumatic to the child. Accordingly, the adult reports of parental behavior and attitudes given by many panic and agoraphobic patients may be descriptions of actual controlling or rejecting behavior by the parent, rather than a distortion created by intrapsychic conflict. Additionally, a child's needy, dependent behavior may induce in certain parents secondary controlling, rejecting, angry behavior. Under various circumstances, then, the parents' empathic failure leads to a failure of the child to internalize structures that modulate intense anxiety.

In a state of fearful dependency, the child becomes angry at the perceived or actual rejecting or frightening behavior of the parent. This anger at the parent leads to guilt, since the parent is also loved, as well as anxiety that angry fantasies will destroy the loved and needed parent. The child will therefore become fearful not only of loss, but of the arousal or expression of anger for fear of loss. Defenses are triggered, including denial and projection, the latter leading to a perception of the parent as even more rejecting. Under certain circumstances, however, the anger at the parent cannot be managed effectively through defensive functioning, and the imagined threat to the parent will escalate to increased fearful dependency and anxiety that the parent will no longer be available for protection. Fearful dependency can therefore lead to the creation of a vicious circle; fearful dependency—anxiety—narcissistic humiliation—anger—guilt—anxiety—fearful dependency.

One result of this pattern can be heightened separation anxiety, in which the child clings to the parent in an attempt to ensure the child's and parent's safety.

The internal representation of significant others as controlling and rejecting may persist into adulthood in such individuals. A sufficiently intense threat to attachment in adulthood will trigger the cycle noted through an increase in regressive fearful dependency. The life events preceding panic, described in the studies noted previously, are perceived by these patients as threats to attachment. In addition to the obvious threat from actual loss or separation, an increase in expectations requiring independent behavior that exposes the individual to the unfamiliar, or change in job or location that takes the individual away from his familiar environment, will also be perceived as threats to attachment. The increased fearful dependency from a sufficiently intense threat to attachment triggers the described escalating cycle, overwhelming the anxiety signal, and a panic level of anxiety occurs. The panic attack decreases the perceived risk to attachment by diminishing the capacity for consciously experienced angry fantasies and feelings and by drawing in the support of others through a plea for help.

Clearly, a conflict between anger and attachment can occur in many different types of psychopathology. Individuals who develop panic disorder, however, appear to have a particularly severe form of this conflict along with a neurophysiological predisposition toward fearfulness. A series of environmental, psychological, and neurophysiological systems may each play a role in triggering and maintaining panic attacks.

Implications for Treatment

The formulation presented suggests that panic patients may benefit most from a treatment that combines neurophysiological, cognitive-behavioral, and psychodynamic approaches. Cognitive-behavioral and psychodynamic approaches overlap to a certain degree in both therapeutic method and mechanism of action.

Bieber (1980) attempts an integration of these approaches when he asserts "that the continued existence of irrational convictions results in the chronic production of false danger signals that set emergency control into operation and that emergency control will continue to respond to false signals until the perceptions of danger arising out of irrational convictions are abolished by a reorientation of these convictions" (p. 15). Weiss and Sampson (1986), in their modification of psychoanalytic theory, give primary importance to pathogenic beliefs in the development of psychopathology. Schwartz (1987) describes a theory of cognition, affect, and learning when he writes that psychoanalytic therapy is "an intricate process of unlearning—a systematic extinguishing of acquired links between cognitive content and affect that involves the examination, reappraisal, and ultimate disregarding of all congruent experiences which have forged these connections and shaped emotional response" (p. 493). Over the course of therapy there occurs "a *reevaluation* of anticipated hazards . . . when familiar threats fail to appear in their expected form . . ." and "a *toning down* of the now inappropriately strident emotional warnings this reappraisal permits" (p. 495).

There is evidence that psychodynamic psychotherapeutic treatment can successfully treat panic symptoms. As we noted previously, several case reports exist of effective psychodynamic treatments. In a series of three case reports by Malan (1979) and one by Mann and Goldman (1982) of successful brief psychodynamic psychotherapy in patients who appear to meet criteria for panic disorder, unacknowledged aggression was seen as the central conflict in this disorder. Making the patient aware of his anger was viewed as a central component of these successful treatments. Milrod and Shear (in press) describe three cases of rapid (approximately six weeks) successful treatment of panic disorder with psychodynamic psychotherapy. In their cases panic disorder appeared to be triggered in the setting of growing independence and intense ambivalent feelings. In follow-up ranging from two to five years, none of the patients had a recurrence of panic disorder. Recent case reports by Silber (1989) and Abend (1989) describe successful treatment of panic attacks during the course of psychoanalysis. Although the treatment of panic was slower in some (not all) of these cases, there is reason to believe that changes in the personality organization resulting from these therapies may lead to decreased panic vulnerability and an alteration in associated characterological difficulties.

Based on the formulation presented here, at least a subgroup of panic patients will be cured of their panic attacks when their sense of inadequate attachment and their intolerance of anger are altered through psychodynamic psychotherapy or psychoanalysis. Future studies of panic disorder may help us to determine which therapy, sequence, or combination of therapies is suitable for which patients. That degree of diagnostic detail is not yet available. The therapist must make a decision as to whether personality problems should take precedence and panic can await relief by psychoanalytic methods, or whether more immediate pharmacological or psychotherapeutic (cognitive-behavioral or, perhaps, brief psychodynamic) treatments of panic should be made while proceeding with further psychodynamic exploration.

More systematic studies, perhaps using manualized versions of psychodynamic psychotherapy, could help to resolve the issue of when psychodynamic approaches alone can effectively treat panic disorder. Construction of such a manual may, however, present certain difficulties because the basis of psychological vulnerability to panic may vary in different cases. Additionally, further studies must be done to evaluate the degree of associated personality disturbances in panic patients before and after treatment of panic, and the degree to which the various approaches to panic (psychodynamic, cognitive-behavioral, and pharmacological) affect the rate of relapse. In our view, these studies will help clarify the role and importance of psychoanalytic approaches to panic.

REFERENCES

Abend, S. (1989). Psychoanalytic psychotherapy. In *Handbook of Phobia Therapy,* ed., C. Lindeman. Northvale, NJ and London: Jason Aronson, pp. 393–403.

Arrindell, W., Emmelkamp, P. M. G., Monsma, A., et al. (1983). The role of perceived parental rearing practices in the etiology of phobic disorders: A controlled study. *Brit. J. Psychiat.*, 143:183–187.

Bieber, I. (1980). *Cognitive Psychoanalysis.* New York: Jason Aronson.

Biederman, J., Rosenbaum, J. F., Hirschfeld, D. R., et al. (1990). Psychiatric correlates of behavioral inhibition in young children of parents with and without psychiatric disorders. *Arch. Gen. Psychiat.*, 47:21–26.

Bowlby, J. (1973). *Attachment and Loss, Vol. II: Separation, Anxiety, and Anger.* New York: Basic Books.

Craske, M. G. (1988). Cognitive behavioral treatment of panic. In *Rev. Psychiat., Vol. 7,* ed. A. J. Frances & R. B. Hales. Washington, D.C.: American Psychiatric Press, pp. 121–137.

Crowe, R. R., Noyes, R., Pauls, D. L., et al. (1983). A family studies of panic disorder. *Arch. Gen. Psychiat.*, 40:1065–1069.

Deutsch, H. (1929). The genesis of agoraphobia. *Int. J. Psychoanal.*, 10:51–69.

Dohrenwend, B. S., Krasnoff, L., Askenasy, A. R., et al. (1978). Exemplification of a method for scaling life events: The PERI life events scale. *J. Health Soc. Behav.*, 19:205–229.

Faravelli, C. (1985). Life events preceding the onset of panic disorder. *J. Affective Disord.*, 9:103–105.

Freud, S. (1895a). Obsessions and phobias: their psychical mechanism and their etiology. *S.E.*, 3.

______ (1895b). On the grounds for detaching a particular syndrome from neurasthenia under the description "anxiety neurosis". *S.E.*, 3.

______ (1926). Inhibitions, symptoms and anxiety. *S.E.*, 20.

Gorman, J. M., Liebowitz, M. R., Fyer, A. J., et al. (1989). A neuroanatomical hypothesis for panic disorder. *Amer. J. Psychiat.*, 146:148–161.

Kagan, J., Reznick, J. S., Snidman, N., et al. (1990). Origins of panic disorder. In *Neurobiology of Panic Disorder,* ed. J. Ballenger. New York: Wiley, pp. 71–87.

Klein, D. F. (1964). Delineation of two drug-responsive anxiety syndromes. *Psychopharmacologia,* 5:397–408.

Korn, M. L., Kotler, M., Molcho, A., et al. (1990). Suicide and aggression associated with panic attacks. Unpublished.

Last, C. G., Barlow, D. H., O'Brien, G. T. (1984). Precipitants of agoraphobia: Role of stressful life events. *Psychol. Rep.*, 54:567–570.

Malan, D. H. (1979). *Individual Psychotherapy and the Science of Psychodynamics.* London: Butterworth.

Mann, J., Goldman, R. (1982). *A Casebook in Time-Limited Psychotherapy.* New York: McGraw-Hill.

Markowitz, J. S., Weissman, M. M., Ouellette, R., et al. (1989). Quality of life in panic disorder. *Arch. Gen. Psychiat.*, 46:984–992.

Marks, I. M. (1970). Agoraphobic syndrome (phobic anxiety state). *Arch. Gen. Psychiat.*, 23:538–553.

Milrod, B. & Shear, M. K. (in press). Psychodynamic treatment of panic: Three case histories. *Hosp. & Comm. Psychiat.*

Parker, G. (1979). Reported parental characteristics of agoraphobics and social phobics. *Brit. J. Psychiat.*, 135:555–560.

Rosenbaum, J. F., Biederman, J., Gersten, M., et al. (1988). Behavioral inhibition in children of parents with panic disorder and agoraphobia. *Arch. Gen. Psychiat.*, 45:463–470.

Roy-Byrne, P. P., Geraci, M., & Uhde, T. W. (1986). Life events and the onset of panic disorder. *Am. J. Psychiatry,* 143:1424–1427.
Sandler, A. M. (1988). Aspects of the analysis of a neurotic patient. *Int. J. Psychoanal.,* 69:317–326.
Schwartz, A. (1987). Drives, affects, behavior—and learning: Approaches to a psychobiology of emotion and to an integration of psychoanalytic and neurobiologic thought. *J. Amer. Psychoanal. Ass.,* 35:467–506.
Shear, M. K., & Fyer, M. R. (1988). Biological and psychopathologic findings in panic disorder. In *Rev. Psychiat., Vol. 7,* ed. A. J. Frances & R. E. Hales. Washington, D.C.: American Psychiatric Press, pp. 29–53.
______ Kligfield, P., Harshfield, G., et al. (1987). Cardiac rate and rhythm in panic patients. *Amer. J. Psychiat.,* 144:633–637.
______ Fyer, M. R., Ball, G., et al. (in press). Sodium lactate vulnerability in panic disorder patients treated with cognitive-behavioral therapy. *Amer. J. Psychiat.*
Sifneos, P. E. (1972). *Short-term Psychotherapy and Emotional Crisis.* Cambridge, MA: Harvard Univ. Press.
Silber, A. (1989). Panic attacks facilitating recall and mastery: Implications for psychoanalytic techniques. *J. Amer. Psychoanal. Assn.,* 37:337–364.
Silove, D. (1986). Perceived parental characteristics and reports of early parental deprivation in agoraphobic patients. *Australian and New Zealand J. Psychiat.,* 20:365–369.
Solyom, L., Beck, P., Solyom, C., et al. (1974). Some etiological factors in phobic neurosis. *Can. Psychiatr. Assoc. J.,* 19:69–78.
Torgerson, S. (1983). Genetic factors in anxiety disorders. *Amer. J. Psychiat.,* 40:1085–1089.
______ (1986). Childhood and family characteristics in panic and generalized anxiety disorders. *Amer. J. Psychiat.,* 143:630–632.
Tucker, W. I. (1956). Diagnosis and treatment of the phobic reaction. *Amer. J. Psychiat.,* 112:825–830.
Weiss, J. & Sampson, H. (1986). *The Psychoanalytic Process: Theory, Clinical Observations and Empirical Research.* New York, London: Guilford Press.

525 East 68th Street
New York, NY 10021

The Clinical and Theoretical Structures of Adult Phobias

JON K. MEYER, M.D. and
VLADIMIR MALETIC, M.D.

AMONG THE CHALLENGES OF WRITING on phobias is the fact that these conditions are among the most dramatic yet commonplace symptoms in psychoanalysis. Everyone has seen or treated someone with a phobia. Unfortunately, there is a tendency to link the commonplace with the clinically trivial. In certain respects, it is as though familiarity has bred contempt. An association of prevalence with simplicity, however, is an assumption that is not justified by the complexity of phobic neuroses or the difficulty in bringing them to a satisfactory resolution.

Along these lines, while phobic symptomatology received prominent mention in Freud's earliest psychoanalytic writings (1894, 1895a,b; Solms, 1989), its complexity and clinical significance was not recognized. Subsequently, however, in the years in which his clinical work and science were maturing, Freud's analysis of phobic symptoms in Little Hans (1909) and the Wolf Man (1918) served, among other functions, to substantiate and defend his concepts of infantile sexuality, to help formulate the castration complex, to set the stage for child psychiatry and psychoanalysis, to emphasize the importance of the primal scene (which became

Dr. Meyer is Training and Supervising Analyst, Chicago Institute for Psychoanalysis; Professor of Psychiatry, Psychoanalysis and Family Medicine, Medical College of Wisconsin.

Dr. Maletic is a Fellow in Psychiatry, Medical College of Wisconsin.

one of Freud's three "primal fantasies"), to introduce his concepts of preoedipal traumata, and to serve as the clinical framework around which he would build his theories of anxiety.

Considering the ubiquity of phobic symptoms, as well as the challenges presented by their analysis, and the difficulties in the way of the patient's recovery, the modern literature has been surprisingly sparse (Moraitis, 1989). Almost 50 years ago, Fenichel (1944a,b) took phobias seriously from theoretical and clinical points of view, and in the following decade there was another flurry of interest (Panel, 1955; Panel, 1959; Wangh, 1959; Greenson, 1959). Since then, while there have been significant contributions, the reports have been scattered and infrequent.

It has been interesting to write this paper because a reconsideration of phobias leads to a reappreciation of some of the most important concepts in psychoanalysis. We have tried to outline and summarize some of those concepts, with particular focus on their clinical application. This paper reflects a clinical and theoretical appreciation of the complexity of the adult phobic construction and of the fact that, for some patients, the analysis of the phobia is the analysis of the neurosis.

Evolution of the Perspectives on Phobias

Despite the prevalence and drama of phobias, their intricacy and the access they provide to fundamental neurotic constructs were not initially appreciated. At first, Freud was uncertain whether phobias had a psychological basis and was inclined—albeit inconsistently—to view them as pure discharges of anxious affect without other content. In that sense, phobias were the paradigm of his first, economic, theory of anxiety. In Freud's early efforts to elaborate a theory of neurosis, he described the precipitating tramatic events as including incompatibilities in the patient's *"ideational life"* (1894, p. 47). In other words, the (prestructural) ego was faced with an experience, idea, or feeling so distressing as to require defensive effort. Freud postulated that the idea could not simply be denied (1894, p. 48) but rather had to be turned from a powerful idea to a weakened one by being converted into something somatic in hysteria or by being separated from its original affect in obsessions and phobias (1894, pp. 51 ff). In 1895 (a), however, Freud distinguished between obsessions and phobias on the basis that obsessions had mnestic and ideational content, whereas phobias did not. In the paper on anxiety neuroses (1895b), Freud combined beautiful clinical descriptions of typical phobic patterns with confusing conceptual distinctions between phobias in which ideational or mnestic content was added, which meant that they belonged to the obsessional neuroses, and phobias associated with anxiety neuroses, which lacked a repressed idea and were ". . . *not further reducible by psychological analysis, nor amenable to psychotherapy*" (1895b, p. 97). Since Freud was a gifted clinical observer before he was a brilliant theoretician, one could assume that the basic clinical observation was that phobic elements were to be found in both obsessional and hysterical neuroses.

In a previously unpublished summary of an early lecture, Freud succinctly stated his position as follows: "With psychological analysis one finds no substitution here, no repressed idea; instead, as the basis of phobias, one only comes across a tendency to anxiety which is psychically further irreducible and which is not influenced by psychotherapy. It is a question of providing information [for the patient] on the source of this tendency to anxiety" (Solms, 1989, p. 93). Nothing could be further from the truth, as Freud discovered.

By the time of Freud's proxy analysis of Little Hans (1909), the concept that phobias lacked ideational content and were irreducible by psychological means was overwhelmed by the richness of the clinical material. Furthermore, it seems fitting that it was in this case that Freud first explicitly used the term, *castration complex* (p. 8), for castration anxiety figured prominently in the analysis of Little Hans and has been generally seen to play a central role in the analysis of phobias ever since. While we need not be overly concerned with Freud's continuing struggles to place phobias in his classificatory system (he considered them to be a part of anxiety-hysteria as distinct from conversion hysteria [p. 115]), it is worth noting the following conclusion, "It seems certain that they [phobias] should only be regarded as syndromes which may form part of various neuroses and that we need not rank them as an independent pathological process" (p. 115). While Freud deemphasized phobias in his nosology, he nevertheless described their dynamics in intricate detail. The contradiction in viewing phobias as contributory rather than as central neurotic elements but describing them with matchless clinical, dynamic, and theoretical elegance may have left subsequent generations of analysts both confused and overawed, contributing to their relative neglect of the syndrome.

In "Totem and Taboo" (1913) Freud made use of his understanding of phobias to generalize from the relationship with the phobic animal (as in Little Hans) to the relationship with the totem animal. The heart of Freud's insight was that the totemic taboos "not to kill the totem and not have sexual relations with a woman of the same totem" (p. 132) coincided with the phobic avoidances that represented repressive efforts directed toward the Oedipus complex. In a part of this paper which is not sufficiently well known, Freud examined the complex interrelationships between a neurotically feared object, as in a phobia, and a neurotically loved object, as in a perversion. He suggested that in terms of the involvement with the object, the fascination with it, and the purpose served in dealing with the castration complex, they are very similar. Since in the unconscious it is an easy transition between love and fascination and fear and avoidance, it would not be surprising if in phobias there would be both avoidance and perverse attachment. Years later, Bornstein (1949) was to describe the perverse elements in a childhood phobia and Ritvo (1966) was to outline their presentation in the same patient as an adult.

As we know, Freud gave up very few of his ideas over the years, tending to modify the circumstances or manner of their application rather than abandon them. While Freud did abandon the idea that phobias were without mental content, he did not entirely abandon the application of suggestion rather than analysis. In 1919, he spoke of the necessity for modification of technique in approaching phobias.

> One can hardly master a phobia if one waits till the patient lets the analysis influence him to give it up. He will never in that case, bring into the analysis the material indispensable for a convincing resolution of the phobia. One must proceed differently. . . . One starts . . . by moderating the phobia . . . and it is only when that has been achieved at the physician's demand that the associations and memories come into the patient's mind which enable the phobia to be resolved [pp. 165–166].

Freud gave the example of a housebound agoraphobic who would, by authoritative suggestion, be converted into one who could walk the streets and thereby come to analysis. Freud's tendency toward suggestion at the time is illustrated in the next paragraph. Fresh from his work with the Wolf Man, he spoke of how a "passive waiting attitude" seemed "even less indicated" in severe obsessional cases. While there is validity to the view that nothing can be analyzed that cannot be brought under analytic scrutiny, authoritative suggestion may create more problems of analyzability than it solves. Clinical discussions continue to contain residues of the idea that the phobic must be forced to confront his fears. Given the highly conflicted impulses and object relationships condensed in that compromise formation, we believe that while some psychotherapy cases may be aided by this expedient, analytic ones may rendered unworkable.

Between and after his major clinical papers, Freud applied his knowledge of phobias to various contexts. For example, their dynamics were utilized to illustrate his arguments in the metapsychological papers on repression (1915a) and the unconscious (1915b), his treatise on the first theory of anxiety in the "Introductory Lectures" (1917), and the formulation of his second theory in "Inhibitions, Symptoms, and Anxiety" (1926). In other words, material from his clinical experience with phobias served as supporting players to other great ideas.

In his most important application, Freud used his two major phobic cases (1909, 1918) as essential clinical material in the reformulation of his theory of anxiety (1926, 1933). In his earliest papers, Freud had assumed that accumulated tension from undischarged sexual energy was directly converted into anxiety in the actual neuroses and was converted into anxiety after repression in the psychoneuroses. Because phobic anxiety seemed so much like a direct discharge, Freud was at first uncertain whether phobias belonged with the actual or the psychoneuroses. Despite the view that anxiety was transformed libido, Freud's study of phobias revealed a close relationship between realistic and neurotic anxiety. Neurotic anxiety was due to internal dangers in the same way that realistic anxiety was due to external dangers. (Later, Anna Freud [1977] would differ from her father, emphasizing the distinction between fear and anxiety. She defined fear as a feeling about real dangers threatening from the outside and anxiety as a feeling generated by internal threats.) He observed that the similarity between internal and external dangers could be used in the creation of a neurotic defense. In the "New Introductory Lectures" Freud commented that an agoraphobic, fearful of an internal sense of temptation while walking on the street, converts that fear into a fear of the street. "What he gains by this is obviously that he thinks he will be able to protect himself better in that way. One can save oneself from an external danger by flight; fleeing from an internal danger is a difficult enterprise" (1933, p. 84).

The concept of anxiety as due equivalently to internal or external danger led to the reformulation of the theory of anxiety and the concept of signal anxiety. As an intermediate step, Freud postulated that automatic anxiety was an internal or external response to a traumatic situation which engendered overwhelming excitement and helplessness in the ego. Signal anxiety was conceptualized as the response of the ego to the *threat* of such overwhelming excitement or helplessness. With regard to phobias, his formulation was that castration anxiety—a realistic anxiety in response to an external danger—forced the repression of libidinal attachments to the mother and the fear of retaliation from the father. Internal danger and attendant anxiety created by the repression was dealt with through condensation and displacement onto the phobic object. The understanding of the symptom as a compromise formation constructed by the ego to express but hide motivation and meaning was yet to be fully appreciated. By the same token, the understanding of signal anxiety as being generated in response to the threat of such awareness and its role in resistance still remained to be fully appreciated.

In the 1940s, Fenichel echoed Freud that fear of the phobic object is a displacement of the anxiety of being overwhelmed by inner excitement. Also like Freud, he noted that the conviction that inner excitement is necessarily dangerous emerges only through the vicissitudes of fears of castration or loss of love. In Fenichel's view, "These deeper forms of infantile anxiety are the very root of the development of the fear that the ego will be flooded with its own excitement . . ." (1944a, p. 287). With regard to the excitement, Fenichel commented: "What is feared by the patient in an enormous excitement of this kind is a breaking down of the ego. . . . It is the loss of voluntary decision which is feared, and it is this loss of control which is represented by a moving vehicle uninfluenced by the wish of a passenger, by a room which cannot be left at will, and also by the mounting sexual excitement approaching orgasm" (1944a, p. 284). In addition to the fear was the fascination integral to the potential loss of control. Fenichel saw the fascination as intensifying the conflict and the anxiety, setting the phobia in motion.

Greenson (Panel, 1959) agreed with Fenichel that the anxiety in phobia is derived from the terror of psychic helplessness. He observed that when the patient reexperiences the original anxiety in the transference, there is a terrifying state of psychic helplessness and loss of ego functions. The raw terror at the heart of phobias may constitute the basis of major transference and countertransference resistances, which may lead to an incomplete analysis. Such incomplete analyses may account, in part, for Weinstock's (Panel, 1959) observation that complete symptom relief occurred in only six out of 46 "completely analyzed" cases and for Moraitis' (1989) comment that the phobic patient will often experience a gradual fading of his fears but the phobias ". . . seldom, if ever, disappear" (p. 234).

While a phobic mechanism projects fear onto an avoidable external object, such mechanisms do not always suffice. Whether the displacements succeed is dependent upon the history and complexity of the entire personality (Fenichel, 1944b). Whereas some anxieties are allayed sufficiently if the patient fulfills the phobic condition—e.g., avoids heights—others expand. The patient may not only be compelled to avoid heights, but also open spaces, bridges, and driving the car. Greenson (1959) made the obvious but important point that while the aim of a phobia is to create new and less frightening dangers and to avoid them through various procedures, this has not worked for the patients seen in treatment. Their phobias do not bind or limit anxiety but instead tend to expand. The fact that such efforts are not effective suggests that more is involved in a phobia than simple displacement and avoidance.

Some of the intricacy in the symptom is accounted for by the close relationship between phobic and counterphobic activity (Fenichel, 1944a). Counterphobic, like phobic, activity is primarily concerned with anxiety control, but is built upon fascination and attraction. While ordinarily anxiety-provoking situations are pursued by the counterphobic, the apparent disregard of danger covers an underlying phobia (e.g., a skydiver who became phobic for heights during his analysis). Such counterphobic situations are not sought because the conflict has been resolved. On the contrary, if this were the case, the counterphobic activity would lose its importance (Fenichel, 1944a, p. 164). The closeness and interchangeability of phobic and counterphobic symptoms parallels and emphasizes the fascination/fear duality in the phobic object.

Jessner (Panel, 1955) noted that phobias defend against both libidinal and aggressive drives. Trying to account for the observation that phobias are found in both hysterical and obsessional neuroses, she suggested that if the defense is primarily against libidinal drives, conversion symptoms or counterphobic enactments may develop, whereas if the danger to the ego is from aggressive drives, an obsessive compulsive neurosis may result. (For an example of a phobia in a hysterical case, see Adams-Silvan [1986], and in an obsessional, see Moraitis [1989].)

In the 1959 Panel, it was agreed that all of the psychic structures contributed to the phobic symptoms. Furthermore, Lewin suggested that "The manifest content of phobias—the psychological equivalent of the manifest dream—should be interpreted according to the rules of dream interpretation" (Panel, 1959, p. 182). The Panel was thus stressing the variety of mechanisms—symbolism, condensation, reversal, metaphor, etc., as well as displacement—employed in the constructions of a phobia. Rubinfine reemphasized the point made earlier by Fenichel, namely, that phobics are not simply avoidant. Rather, "they cling desperately to their primary internal object representations . . . seeking the very object they seem to avoid" (Panel, 1959, p. 184). In fact, Schur observed that libidinization of anxiety makes the phobia difficult to treat (Panel, 1959, p. 184). Although he did not further develop the idea, his comment reflected Freud's interesting comparison between phobia and perversion.

In a separate 1959 paper, Greenson noted that phobias may arise suddenly or gradually, may fluctuate in intensity or remain stable, and may occur singly or multiply (p. 663) and represent unconscious instinctual temptations, either sexual or aggressive or both. He observed that clinically, "Instinctual aims, impulses, or body sensations may be displaced and projected in the phobic situation" (1959, p. 668). Wangh (1959) reiterated that the Oedipus complex was the specific conflict promoting the establishment of a phobia through displacement and projection. He agreed with Greenson that aggressive as well as libidinal strivings were important, a theme echoed earlier by Jessner (Panel, 1955) and much later by Meissner et al. (1987).

In recent papers, Moraitis (1989) stressed the fear of the unknown and narcissism as factors in phobias and their vicissitudes and Sandler (1989) reemphasized the classical view that phobia represents an internal conflict. Sandler added that the selected external object is suitable because it is adapted to symbolically represent the unconscious, conflict-laden fantasy. While superficially the phobic person can avoid the external object to avoid anxiety, Sandler observed, intrapsychically the phobic person needs the phobic object. She described a relationship between the person and the phobic object similar to the fantasied relationship with the original object. For example, when Little Hans's anxiety was strongest he feared (wished) that the horse would come into his room. At times, he also had a compulsion to look at horses, the fright following the compulsion. In other words, the complete phobic syndrome involved not only avoidance of the object but also, at some level, an object relationship.

Clinical Material

Although theoretical constructions are important, theory is incomplete without the substantiation of clinical material. In our experience, phobic features clinically fall into two general categories: (1) phobic manifestations that are part of a symptom complex associated with a hysterical or obsessional neurosis and (2) phobic manifestations that represent the core of the neurosis.

In the first instance, the phobia may rapidly disappear during analysis, with relatively little insight into its genetics or dynamics. Freud may have had experience with such cases in his early clinical work, giving rise to his briefly held views that phobias had no intrinsic mental content. In the second instance, the analysis of the phobia becomes the analysis of the neurosis. In these latter cases, however, the phobia may not be the presenting or even a prominent complaint. For example, in Adams-Silvan's case (1986), treatment was not sought for the phobia but because of more general problems of free-floating anxiety and impulsivity. Nonetheless, the patient's acrophobia was ultimately central to the analysis.

An example of the first type of case was a patient with a hysterical neurosis and agoraphobic symptoms (Meyer, 1988). The agoraphobia was precipitated by the suicide of her mother and served to control anxiety about the oedipal triumph implicit in the suicide. In treatment, the agoraphobia disappeared rapidly without specific attention. It seemed to have been a secondary symptom without substantial roots in the patient's infantile neurosis. The patient, of course, had other deeply rooted symptoms, which were not so easily resolved.

In a case of the second type, an acrophobic traced the origin of his symptoms to being invited by his father to look at his mother's genitalia while the family sunbathed on a roof patio. Moreover, the patient spent hours alone with his mother subathing in the same place. This patient had been obsessional rather than phobic as a child. Looking over the edge of the roof or even sitting hanging his legs over the edge had not troubled him as a child; as an adult, however, his fear was such that he could not even approach the edge. The phobic symptoms had emerged as the patient became more successful in his career and began to seriously contemplate marriage. Unfortunately, although substantial symptom relief was obtained, some elements of the neurosis—particularly some perverse elements—were not resolved and the analysis remained incomplete.

A more completely analyzed case had a phobia to sounds. The man's analysis emphasized not only the condensations, displacements, and avoidances in the phobia, but also the identifications, the fascinations and attractions, and the resistances and defensive impairments of ego functioning.

Seen a number of years ago, the patient was a single, successful businessman in his late twenties, who had grown up in a small town in the West bisected by a single major highway. He sought consultation ostensibly because of a conflict around business decisions. In fact, however, he was anxious, impulsive, sometimes enraged, and worried that he would lose control. His anxiety was palpable, and he felt desperate that his tension, fear, and temper might ruin his life. If the phobia was mentioned during consultation, it was alluded to in such a way as to give little hint of its ultimate central role.

The patient took well to the couch and to free association. He made good use of the analysis to ventilate his enormous anxiety and to provide an outlet for his anger. While he seemed to be clearly an anxiety-hysteric, obsessional mechanisms were also present. As a child and now as an analysand, he found himself debating the meaning of life and his place in it, trying to answer questions that have stumped the philosophers. It was clear that the use of rational arguments to debate the meaningfulness/meaninglessness of life put a capstone on the patient's anxieties and served defensive and resistance purposes similar to those described by Moraitis (1989). It was not clear until much later that this debate also had a meaning that transcended these defensive purposes.

For a period of time the patient's analysis—of anxieties, libidinized affectivity, drive displacements, and obsessional mechanisms—was much like the analysis of any hysteric. Technically, the analysis focused on the patient's resistances, i.e., difficulties in bringing his substantial ego capacities to bear on his own suffering and inhibition. In other words, there was less concern with tracing symptoms to their historical roots than with clarifying the impact of conflict on the patient's ability to think and function. For example, the patient saw the absence of a satisfactory sexual life as the product of a lack of suitable partners rather than as an inhibition generated by conflict. The inhibition was analyzed in terms of its role in controlling anxiety, its function in limiting intimacy, and its influence in restricting consideration of erotic thoughts and feelings rather than in terms of its historical roots. With the analysis of the resistance functions, of course, the genetic and dynamic roots became available.

As the analysis progressed, there was a focusing and narrowing of symptoms, with the phobia being mentioned in passing. The fear was of "coughing sounds," such as coughing, sneezing, clearing one's throat, or blowing one's nose. Also provoking anxiety were associated sounds such as deep breathing, stuffiness, hoarseness, or the rustling of a tissue. Although the patient did not limit his behavior conspicuously enough to draw the attention of friends and colleagues, that was testimony more to his willpower than to the absence of anxiety. And even if he was able to control his avoidances, his activities were stereotyped, constrained, and stressed. Before taking a seat at a table or a position in a room he anxiously examined every situation to identify those people most likely to make the dreaded sounds. Once identified, he maneuvered to distance himself as much as possible from them. When unable to station himself in a protected position, insulated from the sounds and the people who made them, he felt "trapped." Whenever he entered a room, attended a meeting, sat down to a meal, or took a coffee break, he was filled with anxious apprehension that someone would clear his throat, cough, blow his nose, or reach for a tissue, a cough drop, or an antihistamine. Although those around him never seemed to appreciate his turmoil, his emotional state approached terror, on the one hand, and rage, on the other.

If the patient heard a cough, or, worse yet, an attack of coughing, he reacted in a special way. Initially, and only briefly, he would be fascinated with the sound and could imagine feeling all right about it and about the person making it. (He was not bothered by his own sounds, only those of others.) This momentary feeling was followed by a sense of being trapped, a sense of claustrophobic proportions, often close to panic. The feelings were superseded in turn by a murderous rage directed toward the noisy offender. He usually left a particular situation because of the fear of his aggression.

Jessner (Panel, 1955) commented that the precursors of phobia in a child may be a view of the world "as a constant temptation leading to doom" (p. 311). She also remarked that there is a general "discoloring of the outside world, either as a temptation, if the child feels endangered by libidinal drives; or as a destructive place, if aggressive wishes are felt as a threat" (p. 311). When the patient was a child, his world had looked very tempting and certainly filled with doom. Beyond a doubt, he felt endangered from both sets of drive derivatives. The original conscious source of the sounds had been the pleasurable circumstance of having his mother take care of his coughs and colds. He could remember his happy anticipation as she opened her purse and made "rustling" sounds while trying to find a tissue or a cough drop. He also loved it when he had a cough and could stay in bed and get periodic doses of her candy-flavored cough syrup. This situation did not become phobic in childhood; in fact, all he could remember was that these happy circumstances "just ended."

What seemed to replace them was a close, admiring attachment to his father. At about the same time that his happiness with his mother came to an end he was anxiously preoccupied—obsessed—with being compelled to choose between his parents. He "chose" his father with whom he developed a tender, special relationship. He had a fear that his father had taken advantage of this devotion in a sexual way, but in his obsessive rumination he could never decide whether that had occurred.

As a child, the patient lived in a large, rambling house but for reasons of closing off other wings in order to save heat in the winter, his bedroom was situated next to his parents. He developed a childhood fascination with the powerful trucks that rumbled and "coughed" along the highway as they decelerated and accelerated to accommodate to the local speed limit. He walked to the highway, listening for sounds that indicated a semitrailer was coming. As the sound got louder, his excitement and apprehension would increase. When the truck was upon him, he felt the conflict between his fascination and his fear, but they combined into an excitement that kept him rooted to the spot. At night, however, he had a repetitive "truck" dream somewhat different from his daytime experience. In the dream, he could not only hear but also feel the power of the diesel. He was both terrified and fascinated as it came closer and closer. He tried to run away but could only run in slow motion. When it was next to him, the truck left the highway and began to surround him to cut off his escape. He awakened in terror.

Fenichel (1944b) thought that, "It would be worthwhile to study which types of personality, when suffering from neurotic disturbances of concentration, need absolute quiet around them, and which types need external noise" (p. 285). The patient's father was highly sensitive to sounds, demanding that the family remain hushed throughout the evening. Since there were no brothers or sisters to dilute the attention, the requirement of silence was focused on the patient and his mother. Father was particularly irritable when the patient had a cold and sniffles because the sounds were then involuntary and uncontrollable. On the other hand, the patient's father allowed himself to make noise, specifically clearing his throat with gusto and noisily blowing his nose. The father apparently dealt with inner conflict by trying to impose absolute quiet upon the household. In an identification with the aggressor, the patient tried to structure his life so that certain sounds were absent.

As noted previously, Freud (1913) made a useful comparison between phobia and perversion. In phobia the object that symbolizes castration is feared; in perversion, the object that symbolized castration is embraced. In this instance the patient was not an auditory voyeur, he was phobic to sounds. In adolescence, however, he briefly practiced a fetishistic perversion. Freud (1918) indicated that it is important to notice under what conditions the phobia appears; for this patient, the adult phobia consolidated after a period of adolescent perversion when he began to experience passionate feelings for girls.

Greenson (1959) noted that in successful treatment, the original anxiety states are revived in the transference neurosis. "In this phase, the analyst can see how in the acute anxiety state, the loss of ego functions against the person's will, i.e., the loss of memory, perceptions, motility, . . . sense of identity and body integrity, is the most terrifying experience for the phobic patient" (p. 669). In the transference, the patient became sensitive to the analyst's presence and in the place of his more or less controllable phobia, he was panicky at the sound of the analyst's voice. The patient was young and athletic, but his graceful physical control yielded to startling and virtually uncontrollable motions (although confined within the boundaries of the couch) which were a condensation of trying to run away but being frozen in place, of trying to strike out but being held back, and of making both the passive and active motions of sexual intercourse. Although articulate, he developed a paralyzing stammer. He had felt as though he had to choose between loving and hating the sounds and the people who made them: he had to choose. The various mechanisms, particularly the debate on the meaning of life, no longer seemed adequate to control the anxiety. In fact, the debate on the meaning of life was really a question about the uncanny and about entities beyond life. He felt a "presence" in his terror. Was he in touch with someone's essential spirit? Was he possessed by someone? In further analysis, the "possession" was the derivative of his negative oedipal wishes and the sense of the uncanny was the derivative of his castration fears. The patient's reaction contained terror and anxiety but also energy and fascination. There was something precious in his symptoms, and he was not sure that he really wanted to give them up. To give them up would mean to face what he perceived to be the real danger of castration.

Condensed within the phobia was a spectrum of drive derivatives incorporated into the incestuous attachment to his mother, his fear of and identification with his father, the auditory version of the primal scene, the more superficial negative oedipal and deeper positive oedipal conflicts, and the fear of the calamities of childhood and the protection against them. The power of the phobia derived from the patient's fear of his drive derivatives and impulses and the fear of being aware of what he really thought and felt. The anxiety grew not so much from the automatic expression of trauma-generated anxiety as from a powerful signal of danger lest he become aware of his wishes and act upon them. The disruption of ego functions was not a mindless reaction to trauma but a disruption of ego capacities as a resistance to awareness. In terms of his dynamics, positive oedipal wishes accentuated by primal scene experiences were turned by castration fears into a negative oedipal attachment. While childhood heterosexual interest was repressed, angry and rivalrous feelings, auditory primal scene experiences, and fears of retaliation were condensed and displaced onto "coughing" trucks, in a childhood solution that was more counterphobic than phobic. The adolescent perversion attempted to maintain negative oedipal compromises in the face of emerging heterosexual interests. When the latter interests broke through and he became passionately involved with girls, the sound phobia served as a multiply-determined but only partially successful compromise formation.

Conclusion

Phobias are found in individuals with both hysterical and obsessional character structures. Clinical experience indicates that they may be of two types: a transient phenomenon which disappears relatively rapidly in treatment or a complex and highly organized psychopathological formation which is at the center of the neurosis. The analysis of this formation is essentially the analysis of the infantile and transference neuroses.

Phobias are not simply avoidant. There is a relationship or fascination with the phobic object that indicates an attachment to it as well as a fear. In fact, it is the attachment to the phobic object that accounts for its dangerousness and for the fact that avoidance commonly is ineffective. Castration anxiety is central to the development of phobias; it gives rise to a fear of the ego being overwhelmed by its own both libidinal and aggressive excitement.

Phobias are commonplace clinical phenomena, so much so that they earned attention from Freud in his earliest writings. Of the various anxieties he described, the one of relevance in the clinical situation is signal anxiety triggered by the threatened emergence of the meaning and purpose of the patient's conflicts and serving as the motivation for resistance.

REFERENCES

Adams-Silvan, A. (1986). The active and passive fantasy of rape as a specific determinant in a case of acrophobia. *Int. J. Psychoanal.*, 67:467–473.

Bornstein, B. (1949). The analysis of a phobic child. *Psychoanal. Study Child,* 3/4:181–226.
Fenichel, O. (1944a). The counter-phobic attitude. In *The Collected Papers,* Second series. New York: Norton, pp. 163–173.
______ (1944b). Remarks on the common phobias. In *The Collected Papers, Second Series,* pp. 278–287.
Freud, A. (1977). Fears, anxieties, and phobic phenomena. *Psychoanal. Study Child,* 32:85–90.
Freud, S. (1894). The neuro-psychoses of defence. *S.E.,* 3.
______ (1895a). Obsessions and phobias. *S.E.,* 3.
______ (1895b). On the grounds for detaching a particular syndrome from neuroasthenia under the description "anxiety neurosis. *S.E.,* 3.
______ (1909). Analysis of a phobia in a five-year-old boy. *S.E.,* 10.
______ (1913). Totem and taboo. *S.E.,* 13.
______ (1915a). Repression. *S.E.,* 14.
______ (1915b). The unconscious. *S.E.,* 14.
______ (1917). Introductory lectures on psycho-analysis, part III. *S.E.,* 16.
______ (1918). From the history of an infantile neurosis. *S.E.,* 17.
______ (1919). Lines of advance in psycho-analytic therapy. *S.E.,* 17.
______ (1926). Inhibitions, symptoms, and anxiety. *S.E.,* 20.
______ (1933). New introductory lectures on psycho-analysis. *S.E.,* 22.
Greenson, R. (1959). Phobia, anxiety, and depression. *J. Amer. Psychoanal. Assn.,* 7:663–674.
Meissner, W., Rizzuto, A., Sashin, J., & Buie, D. (1987). A view of aggression in phobic states. *Psychoanal. Q.,* 56:452–476.
Meyer, J. (1988). A case of hysteria with a note on biology. *J. Amer. Psychoanal. Assn.,* 36:319–346.
Moraitis, G. (1989). A reexamination of phobias as the fear of the unknown. *Annual Psychoanal.,* 16:231–249.
Panel (1955). Childhood Phobias. A. Benjamin, reporter. *J. Amer. Psychoanal. Assn.,* 3:309–313.
Panel (1959). Phobias and their Vicissitudes. L. Ferber, reporter. *J. Amer. Psychoanal. Assn.,* 7:182–192.
Ritvo, S. (1966). Correlation of a childhood and adult neurosis: based on the adult analysis of a reported childhood case. *Int. J. Psychoanal.,* 47:130–131.
Sandler, A-M. (1989). Comments on phobic mechanisms in childhood. *Psychoanal. Study Child,* 44:101–114.
Solms, M. (1989). A previously untranslated report by Freud of a lecture. *Int. J. Psychoanal.,* 70:91–94.
Wangh, M. (1959). Structural determinants of phobia. *J. Amer. Psychoanal. Assn.,* 7:675–695.

2321 East Stratford Court
Milwaukee, WI 53211

A Clinical Study of a Phobic Illness: The Effects of Traumatic Scars on Symptom Formation and Treatment

BARBARA S. ROCAH, M.D.

FREUD (1926) USED HIS INVESTIGATION of phobias to map the relationship between the generation of anxiety, symptom formation, and the developmental sequence of the danger situation. He concluded that symptomatic and characterological compromises became permanent distortions of the ego to remove the ego from danger of repressed instinctual processes. When the ego is caught off guard and is exposed to a danger that is not mastered through symptom formation, a traumatic neurosis, as opposed to a psychoneurosis, develops. The phobic symptom in particular is distinguished not by its mechanism of formation in response to the unconscious legacies of the infantile neurosis, but by its combination of defenses, which transforms infantile dangers through displacement, regression, externalization, projection, condensation, symbolization, and repression to forms that disguise the wish and the anticipated punishments if the wish were known by the patient and others. The phobic disguise, which Lewin (1952) has likened to the manifest content of the dream, is a deception that retains an unconscious connection to the underlying instinctual

Dr. Rocah is Training and Supervising Analyst, Institute for Psychoanalysis of Chicago.

I am indebted to Drs. Meyer Gunther, Fred Levin, Gordon Maguire, and George Moraitis for reading this paper and offering helpful suggestions. A previous version of the paper was presented at a Panel of the American Psychoanalytic Association on Infantile Sexuality and Its Current Significance for Etiology and Treatment of Neurosis, May, 1987.

issues sufficient to stimulate defensive actions of avoidance.

The case presentation that follows is an effort to rethink the effects traumatic scars have on symptom formation and treatment. My patient consulted me after a previous attempt at psychotherapy had failed to relieve a restrictive airplane phobia, as well as other forms of claustrophobia, panic attacks, and obsessional ideation. The outbreak of symptoms occurred in her late adolescence. Her development had been traumatically scarred by the insufficiency of protective interventions at multiple critical junctures. What was unusual about her adaptation to this strain trauma was a persistent attachment to painful feelings associated with these losses. Pain via identification with her suffering mother, as well as through repetitions of painful sequences of potential loss in the service of belated mastery of trauma, gave her a feeling of object connectedness that was a necessary factor in her adjustment. This attachment to painful affect transcended sensual, unconscious masochistic gratification. Phobias formed the link between memories of past traumas and current maladaptive efforts to provide stability, continuity, and self-guidance through avoidance and projection.

Her phobic symptomatology consisted of three aspects. First, the symbolic symptomatic compromises that were the legacies of her infantile neurosis. Second, deficits[1] in the basic imperatives of adjustment, the scars of her trauma, which threatened her ability to maintain her functioning in the absence of symbiotic partners,

[1]The compromised functional elements in perceptual discrimination, affective monitoring, and mature cognitive functioning that I term deficits, constituted a deviant base for more complex adaptive functioning as she was confronted with new challenges to her capabilities from within and outside the analysis. My use of the term deficit bears a relationship to Abrams' (1986) discussion of impairments in inherent impetus that interfere with the blueprint of development becoming actualized by stimuli in the environment; to Gedo's (1988) term *apraxia,* which defines constitutional or acquired failure to master imperative skills needed for adaptation to reality in the course of development; and to Schafer's (1976) discussion of deformations of personality that are beyond subjectivity and symbolic representation. Schafer mentions factors discussed by Freud (1937), such as inertia, unresponsiveness, agitation, as elements that affect behavior but cannot be considered motives in the same category as wishes, prohibitions, and anxieties.

and phobic avoidance. The third aspect of her illness consisted of characterological responses of negativism, masochism, grandiosity, and entitlement that emerged when her phobic symptoms were threatened and problems in thinking exposed. Phobic symptomatology, in the absence of other regulatory capabilities, provided her with stability, continuity, and guidance.

I am not aware of any literature that discusses a phobia as an example of a traumatic neurosis, the point of view of this paper. The most usual formulation, stated by Freud (1926) and Anna Freud (1977), is that a phobia is an alternative to retraumatization. Others stress isolated ego functions and preoedipal anxieties in relation to archaic objects (Panel, 1958). Brenman (1985) discusses characterological defenses against repetition of traumatic catastrophe that bears some relevance to my work with this patient. Gehl (1973) discusses indecision and claustrophobia. He demonstrates that, following Fenichel (1945), the fear of closed spaces extends beyond actual enclosed spaces, to fear of time, deadlines, decisions, and commitments.

The group of papers most relevant to my thesis deal piecemeal with isolated dysfunctions and dysregulations that form part of the phobic picture that is not subsumed by the conflict-structural model. Noy (1973), Sarnoff (1970) and Renik (1972) have examined cognitive functioning in phobic symbolization and distortion. Schur (1971) highlights two developmental deficits at the center of phobic symptomatology. The first is a distortion of the patient's relationship to reality. There is a failure of the ego to evaluate danger and respond appropriately. The presence of anxiety is used to test reality. This automatic reality-testing is based on infantile mimetic clues and projections that by-pass reflective activity and judgment. Secondly, Schur describes deficits in affect regulation. The anxiety signal is overcome by regressive automatic somatized anxiety. This is presumed to result due to problems in neutralization of anxiety to signal proportions. More recently, Moraitis (1988) has approached the problem of deficits in a different manner. He suggests that the underlying deficit in a phobia consists of a learning disorder in which avoidance can be understood as a fear of novelty. New information from experience and within psychoanalysis is avoided.

The newest research on phobias comes from advances in neurophysiologic knowledge. This research has resulted in a return of interest in the actual neurotic core of anxiety in phobic individuals. Cooper (1985) has reviewed this literature, which he summarizes as follows: Although Freud linked actual neurotic anxiety to dammed-up tension from sexual noxae, more recent formulations have linked actual neuroses to contentless overflow of neuronal excitation that does not originate in a repressed idea. Actual anxiety is not a psychological phenomenon stimulated by phylogenetic anxiety signals of loss and injury. Actual anxiety is a signal of homeostatic disturbance in psychological systems or in neuronal activity. The literature suggests, according to Cooper, that there are some people who are characteristically anxious and phobic with intermittent panic attacks. These people have developed phobic symptomatology largely secondary to a contentless biologic dysregulation manifested by a low anxiety threshold. These conditions have often been linked to mitral valve prolapse, although no direct etiological connection has been discovered. Such patients respond favorably to anti-depressant medication. Psychotherapeutic treatment is used to help the patient undo the learned anticipatory and phobic behavior that developed as magical efforts to cope with panic that is physiologically triggered. Reconditioning attempts to address this issue by teaching new associative connections (Nemiah, 1981).

Although no single case presentation justifies revision of traditional understanding of the syndrome of phobic illness, I believe that there are features concerning this patient that raise questions concerning the relationship of trauma, anxiety, and symptom formation. I am proposing that a phobia is more than a symbolic compromise of infantile dangers, fears of punishment, and adaptation to reality. It is useful to think of phobia as a systemic disease containing an admixture of conflictual, post-traumatic, dysfunctional, and dysregulatory elements, as well as characterological adaptations to these developmental vicissitudes. The significance of any of these factors varies from case to case. Contrary to Freud's (1923) emphasis on punishment or loss as the condition that generates anxiety in relation to drive expression, I am suggesting that the fear of helplessness in a phobia may also be due to the failure to develop functional internal regulatory systems such as the superego, or the ability to transform automatic anxiety to signal proportions. The repetition of the phobia confirms the absence of these functional and regulatory systems. In my patient the phobic patterns themselves emerged as a distorted means of self-regulation that compensated for deficits and characterological problems.

Case Presentation

History

My patient, a 25-year-old, divorced woman, came from a rural Southern background. In addition to an airplane phobia, she suffered panic attacks when she was in closed rooms, and in any vehicle when she was not in the driver's seat. In social situations she exhibited a marked hand tremor, which was a source of great embarrassment. She had numerous obsessional thoughts concerning fears she would do violence to innocent victims. She feared becoming pregnant, the prototype of a decision that could not be reversed. Contemplating abortion aroused anxiety-provoking fears that she was a murderess. She had managed for most of her adult life by clinging to her ex-husband whom she had named her "teddy bear." He had gradually become weary of her demands and left her, saying he wanted an intact partner for a wife. She had been surprised when he left.

Her father was a storefront minister who dominated her mother, a limited, phobic woman with no interests apart from church or home. My patient was the oldest of multiple siblings. Following the birth of the youngest and only boy, when my patient was ten years old, the family entered a prolonged period of disruption and tragedy. Her mother developed a postpartum septicemia and meningitis requiring a three-month hospitalization. My patient, along with siblings and other relatives, kept the household going, including the care of her infant brother, who had been weak and sickly since birth. When her mother finally returned home, her father withdrew the support of relatives in an effort to reengage her in household activities. This proved to be more than her mother could manage. My patient remembered her brother's failure to thrive. She decided that it was her parents' responsibility to care for him rather than hers. She turned her back on what was happening and pursued her personal interests. Following her brother's death when the patient was ten, her mother reclusively retreated from family life. My patient felt responsible and vowed never to have children of her own. Her father, in conjunction with a woman the children called the Admiral, took over the household. My patient began a continuing diatribe against her father for his irresponsible behavior.

Her phobic symptoms began in college. An airplane phobia developed when she attempted to escape the smothering attentiveness of her adolescent sweetheart, who was later to become her husband. She fled from him on an airplane to a distant city for a weekend of fun and flirtation. On her return flight, she imagined his disapproving face when he met her at the airport. He was as she imagined him. He told her she had to choose between being faithful to him or losing him forever. In spite of conscious misgivings about yielding to his threat, she agreed to marry him. In the prolonged period before her marriage she became increasingly avoidant and infantile. Her boyfriend took on the function of guiding her through phobic dangers. Their married life consisted of a smoldering storm that erupted when he failed her need for recognition or protection, and when she avoided sexual intimacy.

She indicated her desperation at the conclusion of her story. She wanted to try a radical "talking cure," although the analytic process loomed as a source of anxiety. She decided to hold off using medication to see what we could accomplish. She felt she was a victim of her parents' pathology. She had tried to escape their internalized influence on two previous occasions: first, before the death of her brother, and later when she tried to include pleasurable sexuality into her life. Based on the failure of these two attempts to escape from her fate, she was uncertain whether the analysis could free her.

Clinical Course of the Analysis

Four dreams demonstrate work in the beginning, middle, and end phases of her prematurely terminated analysis. The first two dreams illustrate conflictual and characterological elements that comprised her illness; the last two dreams demonstrate the post-traumatic deficits and the characterological compensatory structures.

The Opening Phase.

Beginning analysis mobilized an idealizing transference that she characterized as comfortably sitting at my knee and telling me stories she had never told any one before. This image organized a set of memories concerning her mother and herself, unable to sleep, sitting in front of the television set until dozing off. As she grew older, she realized that her mother had used these nightly sessions as means of protecting herself from going to bed with her husband and becoming pregnant again. My patient saw this time as the only private time she had with her mother uninterrupted by her father or other children.

Rather early in her analysis she reported the following dream, "I saw an old man carrying an open book which he was examining intently. I peeked at it and saw it was an art book or a book of pornography. To my surprise, the book turned into a fish that jumped into the water. I tried to catch it with my bare hands, but it escaped." Her initial associations focused on her mother's exhibitionistic displays of sexual subjugation to her father. These scenes dominated the household, and they both repulsed and excited her. She developed two contradictory opinions concerning her mother. On the one hand, she believed her mother's powerlessness in her marriage, on the other hand, she doubted her mother's innocence in her son's death. The patient defended against feelings of uncertainty regarding her own behavior and motives at the time of his death by blaming her parents for what happened. She especially blamed her father for her mother's deterioration.

In childhood she had looked for a way into a relationship with her mother and offered herself as an assistant to her mother's phobic, masochistic, depressed existence. In this dyad, she was the active, assertive, supportive partner. This not only denied her personal needs for care and attention, it put her at risk in her relationship with her father, who preferred women who were submissive and did not threaten his dominance. Her mother had tried to console her feeling rejected by her father by telling her "there are plenty of fish in the sea." This statement became a paradigm for relying upon displacement and substitution as a means of dealing with unpleasant affects and frustration.

Her conscious memories of her father in latency and preadolescence were of games in which she provoked him to chase her. These games appeared to be triggers for repetitive childhood dreams in which she was chased by men and subdued into bondage. She tried to fight off any temptation to submit to her father by imitating his entitlement to fight fire with fire, and not take "no" for an answer. This identification permitted her to keep her distance from him while maintaining her idealization of his pseudostrength, which was an alternative to her mother's masochistic stance. She felt outraged that her father frustrated her oedipal fantasy that she could make him smile better than her mother.

This early dream was not interpreted to the patient. In my view it symbolized both the positive and negative Oedipus that determined the conflictual roots of her illness. In the negative Oedipus she envied her father's sexual access to her mother while she felt exploitively used as mother's birth control and teddy bear. In the positive configuration she portrayed her mother as the fish she competitively wished out of the way and anxiously attempted to retrieve through identification with her mother's helplessness. She felt rebuffed by her father who did not gratify her fantasies of an oedipal victory or care, in her view, about her as a child.

Her confessional outpouring of these memories was allowable within the protective holding environment of the regular analytic appointments. She experienced relief from my nonjudgmental listening and from our jointly paying attention to the mysteries of her childhood that concerned her parents' pornographic relationship, their hidden crimes, and her mother's protestations of sexual innocence. She anxiously questioned me concerning my certainty that she would not throw caution to the winds and go berserk in a shopping center while people looked on helplessly. The feared crowd not only presented opportunities for aggression against innocent victims, symbolizing her brother, mother, and father, it was also an impartial judge who would find her guilty without giving her a chance to justify her actions. She feared doing something again that was as irreversible as her actions at the time of her brother's death. She accepted this initial construction of her lingering sense of responsibility for his death and her phobic avoidance of crowded places.

Over a prolonged period, her confused sexual identity, bisexual illusions, oepidal defeats, and longings to be cared for by me as a child, emerged. She defended against her longings by projection. In the transference she insisted that I, like her father, wished to subjugate her. In this context the following incident took place in which she experienced a panic attack in my office. I had moved my chair away from a draft coming in through the window so that my chair was parallel with her head rather than behind her out of her view. She became anxious, agitated, and pale, and her hands began to shake. She felt I was moving in on her in a threatening manner, that I was accessible to her, and she to me, in ways that frightened her. In the next session we discussed the following dream which helped clarify her response. "I was a satyr. I had a long tail. I remembered when I awoke there were two dogs mating.

They danced around and then they parted." She concentrated on her fixed beliefs concerning men, their entitlements, lusts, and domination of women. Insofar as she recognized sexual excitement within herself, she extinguished it quickly by moralizing that orgasms were obscene since they required her to submit to a man or to her own bodily sensations. She confessed a secret belief that she was more powerful and superior to any man who lusted after her, since they could not control their excitement whereas she could control hers. Any temptation on her part to reexamine her unconscious castrative relationship with men was countered by intensification of phobic behavior followed by regression to a transitional object relationship. In the transference there were negativisitic battles concerning the futility of trying to change.

Gradually we understood that the whole idea of change was linked to her ability to control my participation in her difficulties. She experienced my moving my chair in the previous hour as an intrusion that changed me from a holding mother into her father, exercising my right to do things that affected her without consulting her and without warning. The father transference defended against other longings that were homosexual. She recalled sexual play with girl neighbors in her preadolescence that was satisfying, safe, and exciting, because each of them could walk away from the experience and pretend that nothing happened. We understood that her homosexual fantasies described a wish to control her analytic contact with me. Our relationship should resemble that of the dogs she dreamed about: a mindless, anonymous satisfaction of need and encounter without any meaning other than what she could control, experience as symmetrical, and leave at will. She was frightened of her actual feelings about me: she felt a mixture of dependency, threats to her ability to maintain her separateness from my influence over her, and fears that I would ultimately betray her by losing my mystique of being a man in woman's clothes, and turn out to be a real woman.

To briefly recapitulate the opening phase of her analysis, we observed the following elements. First, an idealizing maternal transference that constituted a holding environment in which she retold memories of confusion, uncertainty, and family tragedies. Second, we reconstructed her fear of crowds as situations in which she was tempted to enact vengeful fantasies on innocent, displaced victims, followed by the crowd judging her without giving her an opportunity for self-justification. Third, we observed sexualization within a father transference that defended against passive longings to be cared for as a young child, and active homosexual wishes of anonymous satisfaction of need and desire without commitment. Fourth, underlying fears of closeness gradually emerged accompanied by fantasies that I would ultimately betray her. Fifth, there was an intensification of phobic symptomatology that occurred when she was tempted to reexamine her perceptual and affective biases.

The Middle Phase.

In the middle phase of her analysis the transference see-sawed between battles in which she fought the fire of analysis with the fire of her negativism, and periods wherein she defended against the emergent homosexual longings in the transference through masochistic provocations. She reported the following dream: "A woman was giving a speech. She suddenly ceased speaking and appeared embarrassed. She turned to the audience and said that she had forgotten a picture she usually carried with her and could not continue speaking until she recovered the picture."

In the course of work on this dream we encountered an aspect of certainty in her thinking that transcended the subjectively organized symbolic meanings that constituted her psychic reality. This certainty was disguised in the dream as dependence upon a hidden transitional picture. She thought the analytic work functioned as a picture in her mind that represented both what she was, and what she might be if she permitted herself to benefit from our work. She wanted to hide any evidence of her dependence upon our work since she believed that I would ultimately betray her. She experienced my interpretations of her negativisitic transference battles as retaliation for her provocativeness. She felt no guilt, she asserted, nor could she see any reason to abandon her belief in her father's version of character strength: to fight fire with fire.

She compared me to a man-in-a-Brooks-Brothers-suit, a man entitled to ignore or debase her because she was a woman. She feared that I would ignore her need for a parent. She had a momentary image of her mother's reproachful face if she used me to free herself. I quickly responded by saying "You wish to share my fate, not your mother's." She explosively responded to what I said by accusing me of speaking for her. "I don't want any human intervention. I have had enough of that! I want a magic wand. Only a wand will cure me. If you can't produce a wand, I will be spiteful."

We understood that no identification with her father in childhood, no idealization of the Admiral housekeeper who came after her mother withdrew, no interpretation that I could offer was strong enough to part her from her participation in her fateful bond with her mother. She demanded a wand, a magic tool, to fix what she essentially viewed as incurable, unmodifiable, and subjectively irresistible. The reasons for this difficult state of affairs gradually emerged. First, it became clear that she was threatened by any disillusionment in her father's advice and by her transference conviction that I could not withstand her aggression. In addition, she experienced the analysis as a danger. She heard our work as another prescription for life that would fail her as badly as the one her parents had given her. I thought by turning a deaf ear on the analysis she hoped that she could hear her own voice, apart from all the prescriptions. This interpretation helped quiet her rage. She began to speak for the first time with despair, rather than anger, concerning the shallow wisdom her parents had offered her. She realized how ill-equipped she was to deal with life as an independent adult. She despaired that there was little to idealize about her parents, and yet she felt inexorably bound to them. Finally, she was uneasy, as was I, about how quickly her rage could be aroused against me. She was uncertain whether she could restrain her desire to extinguish me when I made an error in the face of her certainty that I had done something unforgivable and unforgettable. On the one hand, she was fearful that I would succumb to her rage and she would lose me. On the other hand, by exerting masochistic control over me through demanding that I witness her miserable life and feel guilty, she could coercively draw me into her excited state as a participant. Often she would reproduce the primal screams from her childhood so effectively that patients in my waiting room who overheard her wondered what I was doing to her.

It became increasingly apparent that although much could be explained by understanding the regressive sexual and aggressive conflicts within her phobic symptoms, there were additional issues emerging that did not fall into that category. I have described the mixture of certainty and doubt that emerged in connection with the dream of the lady giving the speech and my interpretation that she wished to ally herself with a powerful figure. We learned that alliances formed in childhood were not wish-fulfillments, but experienced as foreign influences that sadistically demanded her submission to their will. Thus she not only resisted a new alliance with the analyst, she was also unable to reconcile contradictory aims that were associated with internalized aspects of infantile relationships. For example, transference reawakening of her sadism was at odds with her wish to have me function as her teddy bear. Childhood longings to desert her mother's reproachful face were at odds with her traumatic memory of decisions by mother and herself to turn their back on her brother, a decision that, in her view, contributed to his death. Fighting fire with fire was at odds with adult demands for self-restraint, which she felt entitled to ignore. Finally, contained within her negativistic battles was a fierce struggle for autonomy that disavowed her need for human intervention.

The wand was a magic tool to correct what she felt was uncorrectable by human effort. She presented her wish for a wand as a concrete demand in the transference that would expose my ineptitude in providing adequate assistance to her. In childhood she had berated her mother for failing to provide her with a model for her active aims and instruct her in ways of living other than through a symbiotic existence. This was the root of her penis envy. In the transference she berated me for assuming that I was worthy of her idealization and that I could, by interpretive effort, change the course of her life. She saw the wand as a tool that would dispense with her need of a man both as a teddy bear and as a model of privileged existence, as well as the source of lust which she denied herself, except in her dreams. Retrospectively, she viewed her mother's dependence upon her husband as the arena of mother's self-destruction. My patient gradually realized that her own battles over sex with her ex-husband and other men had been a belated attempt to save her mother in fantasy.

As a result of this work, she experienced less need to prove her strength through sexual renunciations. In this realm she could achieve some distance from her bondage to her mother and pursue sexual relations as long as they were mutual and she could freely exercise her right of refusal. However, this emotional distance from her mother did not stem the full tide of her envious existence. The second meaning of the wand emerged in the transference as she protested what she experienced as the inequity of her patient status as compared to my doctor status. This inequity was similar to what she experienced on airplanes where she was surrounded by people who, she imagined, had a better life than she had. It turned out that she avoided airplane travel, not because of what the plane symbolized, but out of fear that she would fly into uncontrollable rage in the presence of privileged passengers who would judge her harshly and unfairly. Only a wand, in her view, could correct the conditions that underlay the rage.

The patient and I searched for ways to cope with the complexity of her character structure. It was not the content of her fantasies, wishes, and fears that was extraordinary. What was extraordinary and unexpected was the vehemence of her demands, the rigidity of her perceptions, the spitefulness that characterized her response when frustrated or when I made an error, and the aggressiveness and tenacity of her suffering. These responses appeared to entrap her in a mental prison from which there was no escape other than through magical illusions. Repetitive sequences of negativisitic panicky storms that followed each piece of understanding led me to shift my technique from listening to her unconscious motives, defenses, and anxieties, to a new focus on how she processed information. I began to address the rigidity in her thinking processes. These processes were sometimes so rigidly maintained that self-reflection was impossible. I stopped chasing her with interpretations that she sometimes listened to, sometimes assimilated, and sometimes resisted with vehement outpourings of rage. In the dialogue we appeared to repeat the chase games of her childhood. I responded to her reckless behavior in the hours by confronting her with the discrepancy between her desire to have me be helpful to her and her assaults on me, which threatened to destroy my effectiveness with her. I thought her panic in the sessions was the outcome of her insistence on irrational behavior, such as I have described, which inevitably meant frustration, since she could not achieve her irreconcilable ends. I attempted to offer instruction in my way of conducting a dialogue other than through her insistence on her entitlement to turn a deaf ear on the voice of reason. These efforts "beyond interpretation"[2] (Gedo, 1979) enabled us to look, for example, at her envious feelings both in the analysis and outside. She realized that envy was not the outcome of a biological given, but her response to things she observed, some of which were truly enviable to her; others were fatuous and stereotypic, and still others concerned beliefs that were the outcome of her projections of her wishes into other people. She gradually comprehended that her envious rage attacks were triggered when she was frustrated in her attempts to seduce or woo someone to her point of view. This repeated her childhood

[2]I trust that my clinical illustration clarifies that interventions beyond interpretation are designed to foster, deepen, and deal with the analytic process as it reaches into those aspects of mental life, development, and behavioral regulation not subsumed by the conflict-structural model. As Gedo has asserted (1979, 1981, 1988) patients who enter the oedipal area hampered in basic psychological skills, as I believe this woman was, cannot resolve their pathology by either interpretation in the realm of symbolic subjectivity, symptomatic and characterological manifestations, or through the provision of empathic understanding alone. Rather, the deficient skills need to be directly confronted through technical methods that isolate them and bring them into the work. (See also Eissler, 1953.)

attempts of insisting that she alone could successfully bring a smile to her father's lips. Eventually she began to mourn her oedipal father, who frustrated her attempts to seduce him.

The End Phase.

Out of persistent work in the manner described, her capacities for reality testing, discrimination, and judgment improved. Examination of her envious relations with men eventually permitted work surrounding her identity as a woman and reflection upon her claims for bisexual perfection in herself (as in her dream of a satyr, and her wish for a wand). The seductiveness of her father's entitlements, which offered an alternative to her mother's symbiotic existence, had led to an idealization of him and repeated attempts at mastery via masculine identification and rejection of femaleness. However, our ability to sustain this effort collapsed in connection with the following dream.

"I was with a friend and her husband. They were having a fight. Her husband was atypically fighting back. My friend turned to me and said, 'Don't bother about him, he's drunk.' Then I was with you and your husband. He supported you against my spiteful attacks." She described her friend as a domineering woman married to a man who was under her thumb. She said her dream had been stimulated by observing me, after her previous hour, laughing while I was speaking with a male friend. She laughed and said that in her dream she blew off my good mood by making me drunk and angry. She had felt excluded by my conversation with my friend. She entertained spiteful fantasies of ruining my pleasure in my work by remaining sick. She demanded that I provide her with compensation for her misery by giving her medication. She said that remaining sick would insure that neither her parents nor myself would be relieved of guilt about her wasted life. We understood that psychotrophic drugs were a magic wand that would automatically take care of thinking and reacting without her having to pay attention to my instructions. I said I thought her dream image of my needing help from my husband ruined me as a person worth listening to. I further interpreted that she was attempting to resolve her uncertainty in the transference concerning her perceptions of me and my worth to her by throwing caution to the winds and making statements concerning vengeance, spoiling, and Pyrrhic victories. She impeached me on the grounds that I was dependent upon a man for pleasure and protection. She felt I was no different from her mother. Her interest in me had been defined by her fantasy that I was a man dressed in women's clothes, a perfect bisexual being. At the end of this interpretive work she briefly debated whether she should continue with the analysis in the face of her disillusionment in me. She thought she needed medication. She felt that since I regarded her rages and entitlements as illusions of masculine strength rather than real strength, I was of no help to her.

We had long understood that these character traits of rage and entitlement had offered a means of survival in the face of endless temptations for regression to masochism and symbiosis. Now it seemed clear that her dependence upon suffering and pain, not the rages that defended against her suffering, were the problem that needed to be addressed. She felt overwhelmed, within the transference, to act out her vengeful fantasies toward me. She elected to withdraw from analysis.

Following prolonged discussion she went for a consultation for medication. She looked upon antidepressants as an authority that would not betray her in ways she felt I had in the transference. The drug by-passed her subjective wishes for vengeance and conflicts about relinquishing masochistic control over the environment. She left analysis with her phobias intact, expressing regrets that we had not succeeded. She acknowledged my efforts to help her. She prided herself on being able to walk away from me. About eight months after we interrupted, during which time she had been on medication and feeling better, she returned to attempt to work out a more satisfactory ending. After a few weeks she felt flooded with rage and reproaches. We agreed to stop. She confessed that she never believed the analysis would be successful. She had demanded a wand because my actions convinced her that no human intervention could live up to her expectations and undo the effects of the past.

DISCUSSION

The case material can be discussed from several viewpoints. I will use the concept of a traumatic neurosis to account for the structure of her illness and the repetitions of phobic patterns. In addition to the threat of retraumatization within a symbolically encoded wish, fear of punishment, and exposure to an idiosyncratically organized danger situation, I have inferred from this analytic work that retraumatization can also threaten when an individual is exposed to situations that reawaken nonsymbolic states of tension.[3] This seemed to be the case when my patient was exposed to situations in which her cognitive-perceptual discriminatory-affective monitoring systems were overtaxed relative to the strength of repressed wishes. The imbalance led to enactments when her environment failed to support her ability to discriminate between illusion and fact or failed to provide unassailable moral reliability. In this particular patient the clinical picture was complicated by characterological expressions of grandiosity, entitlement, and negativism, which functioned to compensate for deficits and to disavow her dependency upon human partners, as well as the necessity to submit to reason.

I am suggesting that an individual learns to mediate anxiety through establishing what Emde (1988)[4] terms a matrix of coor-

[3]Stern (1988) states: "Signal anxiety indicates that the subject has developed the capacity to utilize his states of tension as signals of danger. This must mean that he has acquired the ability to attribute meaning to those states of tension, where such ability was absent in the past. This ability is the precondition for movement from unpreparedness or passivity (trauma) to preparedness or mastery" (p. 102).

[4]Emde (1988) suggests that when these coordinations are brought into play they facilitate development of later structures: consolidation of affective core of self, a sense of reciprocity, rules, and empathy, and aspects of early moral internalizations (prohibitions), and an executive sense of we in the context of positive emotions. These structures were compromised in this patient.

dinations with the environment. These include cognitive maturation, perceptual discriminations, action potentials, intersubjective communications, and affective monitoring. The phobic attack appears to represent the endpoint in a sequence that begins with a state of tension that is inadequately regulated by these adaptive capacities. Symbolic meaning is gradually attached to this tension disturbance followed by defensive and characterological compensations. Avoidance of the danger situation in which the meaningful or presymbolic state of tension is aroused is part of a learned solution to deal with problems in internal regulation (Cooper, 1985; Stern, 1988).

Whether the presence of functional deficits requires variations in technique has been widely written about and debated. The discussion centers on whether to view these problems as compromise formations that require analysis of component parts (Brenner, 1979; Gediman, 1984; Coen, 1986; Boesky, 1988), or to conceptualize them as distortions of development that limit the psychoanalytic project of revision and require the introduction of parameters to deal with the clinical picture (Freud, 1919, 1937; Eissler, 1953). Radical revisions of clinical theory to deal with these problems have been proposed (Winnicott, 1963; Kohut, 1971, 1984; Kernberg, 1975; Gedo, 1979; Model, 1985; Moraitis, 1988).

Gedo (1979, 1981, 1988) has dealt systematically with maladaptive behavior that results from nonconflictual causes and its imbrication with conflictual elements. He discusses deficits as functional disorders that he terms apraxias, which are based on a failure to acquire "know-how" in or out of the analytic setting that can free an individual from the need for a symbiotic mode of adaptation. His ideas were useful to me in assisting my thinking about my patient's tendency to collapse into states of panicky helplessness, defensively screened by her negativism, masochism, grandiosity, and entitlement. Analytic work, focused on penis envy and her grandiose illusions of acquiring superiority to men by denying herself sexual desire and satisfaction, involved not only understanding her identification with her father's entitlement and the risk that placed on her identity as a woman, it also involved working with her capacity for reality testing, her ability to acknowledge boundaries, to make perceptual discriminations, and to acquire some ways of monitoring her affect within a dialogue. These apraxic elements had necessitated her reliance on either phobic symptoms or upon a symbiotic partner who acted as an external guide through danger. Eventually, she partially accepted the idea that some compromise and submission were part of normal existence and possible for her in sexual relations.

In Kohut's self psychology (1971, 1984) deficits are at the center of psychopathology, in contrast to Gedo's view. Kohut sees the aim of psychoanalytic intervention to reestablish linkages and integration between the unaltered, preconscious, thwarted aims of a developing self and the more realistic, goal-striving aspects of the central personality. These integrative failures are, in his view, overcome through the action of the empathic selfobject analyst, who restores lost self-integration by understanding and explaining transference ruptures in empathy. The presented case material can be looked at from this point of view: The strident aggression and masochistic sexuality that she demonstrated might be understood as epiphenomena within a vulnerable failing self no longer sustained by the available presence of a mediating, idealizable selfobject analyst. It is interesting to note that although an idealizing transference was established at the beginning, it could not be maintained in the face of disillusionment in me in spite of efforts to understand and restore it. Attempts to work through the ruptures that occurred seemed to excite her more than calm her. My acknowledgment of breaks in empathy only confirmed for her that I was impeachable and fallible and therefore not worth listening to. This intensified her search for an idealizable perfect being. Threatened by transference disillusionment in my worth and by the consequences of maintaining her phobic symptoms, she claimed she needed either a magic wand or medication to release her from suffering. Medication, in my view, seemed to substitute for the mediating, temporary benefits of an idealizing transference. It appeared to strengthen her level of integration when she experienced tension through decreasing the intensity of her affects. She could then use the assimilative and judgmental capacities available to her rather than depend upon phobic avoidance or a symbiotic partner.

Moraitis (1988), from a totally different perspective, addresses what he terms the phobic patient's fear of novelty. In an interesting paper, he advocates interventions that acknowledge both the patient's and analyst's awareness of ignorance and uncertainty such that novel hypotheses can be generated. This idea is relevant to my work with this patient who had such an extreme reaction when she thought I spoke for her and interpreted her wish to share my fate, not her mother's. This statement produced a crisis in the analysis. I have understood this crisis as experiencing her fear of depending upon her own judgment or that of imperfect human partners. The absence of unimpeachable authority in her background constituted a serious environmental deficiency, which affected her relationship to learning and to authority. Her phobic symptoms functioned as an unimpeachable authority. They removed her from danger. They organized her perceptions in ways that seemed infallible to her. They set rules and frames of permitted activity. They substituted for ethical authority.

It seems reasonable to infer that there is a spectrum of constructs included in the phobic disorder that includes neurotic elements, dyadic problems, trauma-induced failures of regulation of states of excitement and affect, and archaic cognitive functioning. Within this illustrative clinical material these constructs constituted, clinically useful vantage points from which to examine phobic illness rather than separate diagnostic entities in which phobias appear or sometimes predominate.

None of these constructs, however, address what is perhaps the most unusual feature of this clinical picture: the attachment to painful feelings as an organizer of traumatic experience. Freud (1920) stated that the symptomatic picture of the traumatic neurosis approached that of hysteria, but surpassed it in its marked signs of subjective pain, as well as in evidence of general enfeeblement and disturbance of mental capabilities. He used the concept of traumatic neurosis to discuss repetitions that were not governed by the pleasure principle.

The repetitions that comprised this patient's illness were of two types: first, a search for recognition and awareness of herself in familiar contexts, even when those necessitated the repetition of traumatic features (Emde, 1988; Moraitis, 1988). Second were repetitions motivated by belated mystery of traumatic helplessness (Freud, 1920). These attempts consisted of reversal of passive into active, identification with the aggressor, blaming, and self-justification. Her panicky states recreated the threat of loss of a reproachful, but necessary tie to her mother who functionally abandoned her in childhood. Loss of her mother left her flooded with painful affects, confused about making choices, mindless of the consequences of her actions, unable to fathom the contradictions she witnessed in her environment, and abandoned to make do with other fish in the sea as a substitute for maternal care and rejection by her father, who did not see her as a child in need of help. Each phobic repetition affirmed her connectedness to the past, and established new, current witnesses to her suffering, and through identification, to her mother's suffering. Each phobic repetition was a memorial to the past that reassured her she had not released her parents from their responsibility for her illness. Rather than the vicissitudes of her development becoming relegated to the realm of remembered predispositions, they remained at the level of repetitive enactments.

The specific attachment to pain as an organizer of her mental life transcended sensual masochism. Valenstein (1973) suggests that children can become attached to pain when there is failure to establish consistent and constant relationships with a positively valued object. Inconsistency of this sort does not lead to consolidation of pleasurable affect as an anticipatory signal. Rather the opposite prevails: the development of an affinity for painful affect, the memorial to the inconsistent pleasure-pain yielding relationship. We reconstructed that she had attempted, as a child, to gain what pleasure she could from lending herself to her mother's exploitive use of her as a symbiotic partner. Identification with maternal depression and suffering alternated with repetitive sequences enacted with the father of excited arousal admixed with fears of further entrapment. Her preoedipal sensual attachment to pain and pleasure was symbolically represented in oedipal chase dreams in which she was both the victim, forced to submit, and the seductress who could unconsciously engage her father in forbidden activity (Lowenstein, 1957). Pain also represented a form of object tie other than a sensual one. She experienced renunciation of pain as a potential loss of control over the environment. Control was exercised through engaging witnesses to her suffering. This provided belated mastery over the childhood circumstances surrounding her brother's death. At that time there were no unselfish witnesses to his deterioration and no people to monitor her choices and actions that led, in her view, to such fateful consequences.

Ultimately she longed to be emancipated from her mother's fate. Paradoxically, she resisted analytic efforts to revise her bond to her mother and the past. This resistance was not due, in my opinion, to a negative therapeutic reaction and sadistic superego. In fact, the absence of a reliable internalized moral authority constituted a serious vulnerability in her character structure. Her resistance to new adaptation was better accounted for by understanding that suffering, pain, and vengeful fantasies were necessary aspects of her survival. She felt she must be strong to have survived so much. This conviction satisfied self-esteem requirements and was the remnant of her nuclear self (Kohut, 1984), which, in her view, needed to be protected from any and all impingements.

Under these circumstances, the analysis could not really succeed, no matter how heroic the analytic efforts to address multiple aspects of her personality. This she acknowledged as the end of our work. She determined she needed to leave the analysis when a demand for some rational behavior was engaged within the analytic work itself: some sense of an executive we and collaborative effort (Emde, 1988) and tolerance for ambiguity and error on her part or mine (Moraitis, 1988). Resistance was greatest against the awareness of the implications of the damaged structure of her personality, the outcome of trauma. These developmental vicissitudes had been incorporated into symbolic meanings, but not extinguished by them.

In general, this woman resisted new influence within the analysis. Freud (1919) was outspokenly pessimistic concerning the ability of phobic patients to make use of insight that addressed only symbolic encoded meanings and compromise formations. He advocated active techniques in which the person needed to face the phobic situation directly in order for resistances to recovery to yield to insight. It was our attempt to confront the resistances to synthesize new information within the analysis that led to the interruption. The interruption indicates that the capacity to rethink and reprocess information anew is pivotal in the effort to face the phobia within the analytic work itself, and resistances to that process are not necessarily derived from conflictual sources (Eissler, 1953).

A phobia is more than a neurotic compromise. The compromise does subsume dysfunctional and dysregulatory deficits only insofar as it acts as a pathological regulator of a person's disordered existence. The fixity of a phobia can be attributed to more than a continuing struggle against repressed instinctual influences. Lifting repression in this patient resulted in an exaggeration of symptoms and character defenses. This was explained by an organization that was beyond the pleasure principle: a traumatic neurosis that predisposed to repetitions in the service of belated mastery of trauma and predispositions to repeat familiar contexts. The rigidity was secondary to the presence of dysregulatory and dysfunctional capacities that interfered with new assimilations and accommodations taking place.

REFERENCES

Abrams, A. (1986). Disposition and the environment. *Psychoanal. Study Child,* 41:41–61).

Boesky, D. (1988). Comments on structural theory of technique. *Int. J. Psychoanal.,* 69:303–317.

Brenner, C. (1979). Working alliance, therapeutic alliance, and transference. *J. Amer. Psychoanal. Assn.* (Suppl.), 27:137–157.

Brenman, E. (1985). Hysteria. *Int. J. Psychoanal.,* 66:423–433.

Coen, S. (1986). The sense of a defect. *J. Amer. Psychoanal. Assn.,* 34:47–69.

Cooper, A. (1985). Will neurobiology influence psychoanalysis. *Amer. J. Psychiat.,* 142:1395–1402. Eissler, K. (1953). The effect of the structure of the ego on psychoanalytic technique. *J. Amer. Psychoanal. Assn.,* 1:104–144.

Emde, R. (1988). Development terminable and interminable. II. Recent psychoanalytic theory and therapeutic considerations. *Int. J. Psychoanal.*, 69:283–297.
Fenichel, O. (1945). *Pssychoanalytic Theory of Neurosis*. New York: Norton.
Freud, S. (1919). Lines of advance in psycho-analytic therapy. *S.E.*, 17.
_____ (1920). Beyond the pleasure principle. *S.E.*, 18.
_____ (1923). The ego and the id. *S.E.*, 19.
_____ (1926). Inhibitions, symptoms and anxiety. *S.E.*, 20.
_____ (1937). Analysis terminable and interminable. *S.E.*, 23.
Freud, A. (1977). Fears, anxieties and phobic phenomena. *Psychoanal. Study Child*, 32:85–91.
Gediman, H. (1984). Actual neurosis and psychoneurosis. *Int. J. Psychoanal.*, 65:191–203.
Gedo, J. (1979). *Beyond Interpretation*. New York: Int. Univ. Press.
_____ (1981). Measure for measure: A response. *Psychoanal. Inquiry*, 1:286–316.
_____ (1988). *Conceptual Issues in Psychoanalysis*. Hillsdale, NJ: The Analytic Press.
Gehl, R. (1973). Indecision and claustrophia. *Int. J. Psychoanal.*, 54:47–61.
Kernberg, O. (1975). *Borderline Conditions and Pathological Narcissism*. New York: Aronson.
Kohut, H. (1971). *The Analysis of the Self*. New York: Int. Univ. Press.
_____ (1984). *How Does Analysis Cure?* Chicago: Univ. Chicago Press.
Lewin, B. (1952). Phobic symptoms and dream interpretation. *Psychoanal. Q.*, 21:295–322.
Loewenstein, R. (1957). A contribution to the psychoanalytic theory of masochism. *J. Amer. Psychoanal. Assn.*, 5:197–234.
Modell, A. (1985). The works of Winnicott and the evolution of his thought. *J. Amer. Psychoanal. Assn.* (Suppl.), 33:113–139.
Moraitis, G. (1988). A re-examination of phobias as the fear of the unknown. *Annual Psychoanal.*, 16:221–249. New York: Int. Univ. Press.
Nemiah, J. (1981). Psychoanalytic view of phobias. *Amer. J. Psychoanal.*, 41:113–120.
Noy, P. (1973). Symbolism and mental representation. *Annual Psychoanal.*, 1:125–158. New York: Quadrangle Press.
Panel (1958). Phobias and their vicissitudes. *J. Amer. Psychoanal. Assn.*, 7:182–192.
Renick, O. (1972). Cognitive function in phobic symptoms. *Psychoanal. Q.*, 41:537–556.
Sarnoff, C. (1970). Symbols and symptoms: Phytophobia in a two-year-old girl. *Psychoanal. Q.*, 39:550–562.
Schafer, R. (1976). *A New Language for Psychoanalysis*. New Haven: Yale Univ. Press.
Schur, M. (1971). Metapsychological aspects of phobias in adults. In: *The Unconscious Today*, ed. M. Kanzer. New York: Int. Univ. Press.
Stern, M. (1988). *Repetition and Trauma: Toward a Telenomic Theory of PSychoanalysis*. Hillsdale, NJ: The Analytic Press.
Valenstein, A. (1973). On attachment to painful feelings and the negative therapeutic reaction. *Psychoanal. Study CHild*, 28:365–394.
Winnicott, D. (1963). Psychiatric disorders in terms of infantile maturational processes. In: *The Maturational Processes and the Facilitating Environment*, 1965. New York: Int. Univ. Press.

111 N. Wabash
Chicago, IL 60602.

The Evolution of Freud's Conceptualization of Phobias

DAVID S. SPIRA, M.D.

THE PURPOSE OF THIS ARTICLE is to review the evolution of Freud's understanding of phobias, with a particular eye toward the distinction he made between actual neuroses and psychoneuroses. This focus is relevant to the question of biologic versus psychologic factors in producing pathology. Because the subject of phobias occupies a central position in psychoanalytic theory by virtue of its intimate relation to an understanding of anxiety and defense, the reciprocity between Freud's evolving models of mind and his ideas on phobia will also receive attention.

This review is organized in accordance with the three major phases of Freud's theorizing. During the early phase, which lasted until 1905, he thought phobias were caused by traumatic events and their associated affects. Phase two, from 1905 to 1923, was characterized by his rejection of the seduction hypothesis and the development of the libido theory. Working within the context of the latter, Freud described two forms of phobia, one emphasizing a psychogenic mechanism, the other, designated as actual neurosis, explained by an accumulation of libido—a cumulative biologic factor. Phase three follows the introduction of the structural model with the publication of "The Ego and the Id" in 1923, which paved the way for Freud's final major reconsideration of phobias

Dr. Spira is on the faculty of the Institute for Psychoanalysis of Chicago.

in 1926 where the emphasis fell on the defensive operations of the ego, especially on signal anxiety.

To make a sharp distinction between biologic and psychologic mechanisms in Freud's understanding of phobias may be misleading. Freud thought that psychological events would ultimately be found to be based on biology and could be accounted for in the concept of drive. A review of Freud's work, however, reveals a lack of clarity about exactly how phobias were to be explained, especially agoraphobia, as he grappled with the question of whether it should be understood as a psychoneurosis or an actual neurosis. This question essentially refers to the place of defensive operations and the transformations of symbolic meaning in the development of the phobic symptoms. Strachey (1962, pp. 83–84) in his Appendix to Freud's paper on "Obsessions and Phobias" (1895) alludes to this equivocality.

In the first phase Freud thought that an event that produced a distressing affect was repressed, preventing the discharge of affect and leading to the phobia—Freud called them "strangulated affects." Anna O., for example, suffered for a time from hydrophobia. "During hypnosis it turned out that she had once unexpectedly seen a dog drinking out of a tumbler of water of hers' (Freud, 1893, p. 33). The affect of disgust was associated with the event and formed part of the phobic complex. The cathartic method of treatment evolved in relation to this theoretical model and aimed to free the strangulated affect through abreaction produced by the use of hypnosis and, later, free association. Freud (1893) thought (p. 36), "The increase of the sum of excitation takes place along sensory paths, and its diminution along motor ones." When discharge is prevented, the result is a neurotic symptom.

In 1894 Freud described the mechanism of symptom formation in hysteric conversion and phobias. In hysteric conversion, affect attaches to somatic innervations, whereas in phobia the affect attaches to other *ideas*—it remains *"in the psychical sphere. . . .* This, in a few words, is the psychological theory of obsessions and phobias . . ." (p. 52).

Freud comments (p. 54) that affect can attach to any idea,

although among the ideas most generally affected it "will seize upon the common primary phobias of mankind about animals, thunderstorms, darkness, and so on, or upon things which are mistakenly associated . . . with what is sexual—such as micturition . . . and contagion generally."

Phobias result from a need to avoid evoking the memory which the ego endeavors to keep unconscious. The theory of therapy relevant to this model involves discovering the source, i.e., the traumatic event and its associated affect, making this unconscious complex conscious, thereby relieving the strangulated affect, resulting in phobia resolution. On an economic basis, the displacement of "a quota of affect or sum of excitation" (1894, p. 60) underlies the theory of abreaction. At this time any distressing experience was theoretically capable of inducing a phobic symptom, although Freud soon considered sexual excitations among the events most likely to produce such disorders.

An important theoretical transition occurs when (Freud 1895) asserts that phobias are in fact "actual neuroses." Freud had first stated his position on the relationship of certain phobias to the actual neuroses in 1894 when he asserted that "The group of typical phobias, of which agoraphobia is a model, cannot be traced back to the psychical mechanism described above; on the contrary, the mechanism of agoraphobia differs from that of obsessions proper, and of the phobias that are reducible to them, in one decisive point. There is no repressed idea from which the anxiety affect might have been separated off. The anxiety of these phobias has another origin" (pp. 57–58m).

Freud asserts that in the phobias "Substitution is no longer the predominant feature . . . psychological analysis reveals no incompatible, replaced idea in them. Nothing is ever found but the *emotional state of anxiety* which, by a kind of selective process, brings up all the ideas adapted to become the subject of phobia. In the case of agoraphobia, etc., we often find *the recollection of an anxiety attack;* and what the patient actually fears is the occurrence of such an attack under the special conditions in which he believes he cannot escape it" (pp. 80–81).

Freud continues: "The anxiety belonging to this emotional state, which underlies all phobias, is not derived from any memory; we may well wonder what the source of this powerful condition of the nervous system can be." He then argues for the distinction of anxiety neurosis, one of the actual neuroses, possessing no psychical mechanism and originating from an "accumulation of sexual tension . . ." resulting from disturbed sexual practices. He maintains that "Phobias, then, are *a part of the anxiety neurosis*" (p. 81); and concludes by pointing out that phobias and obsessions may occur together and that this is a "very frequent occurrence" (p. 82).

Which brings us to consider the relationship between phobias and obsessions. What does Freud mean when he refers to the phobias that are "reducible" to obsessions? How is it to be decided whether certain fears are to be classified as phobias or as obsessions with accompanying anxiety?

Freud (1895) asserts that "Obsessions and phobias are separate neuroses. . . . Two constituents are found in every obsession: (1) an idea that forces itself upon the patient; (2) an associated emotional state. Now in the group of phobias this emotional state is always one of 'anxiety', while in true obsessions other emotional states such as doubt, remorse, or anger, may occur just as well as anxiety" (p. 74). It appears that the affect is a critical element in the distinction. "In many true obsessions it is quite plain that the emotional state is the principal thing, since that state persists unchanged while the idea associated with its varies." Elaborating further: "People who doubt have many doubts at the same time or in succession. It is the emotional state which remains constant in them; the idea changes" (p. 75). In obsessions, the original idea is replaced by a substitute and the motive is "an act of defense of the ego against the incompatible idea" (p. 79). (This description of the mechanism of obsessions, however, sounds more like that which will later be employed in an understanding of phobia.)

Freud distinguishes two groups of phobias "according to the nature of the object feared: (1) common phobias, an exaggerated fear of things that everyone detests or fears to some extent: such as night, solitude, death, illness, dangers in general, snakes, etc.; (2) contingent phobias, the fear of special conditions that inspire no fear in the normal man; for example, agoraphobia and the other phobias of locomotion. It is interesting to note that these phobias have not the obsessive feature that characterizes true obsessions and the common phobias. The emotional state appears in their instance only under special conditions which the patient carefully avoids" (p. 80).

Phase two was heralded by the publication of the "Three Essays on the Theory of Sexuality" (1905) and Freud's public rejection of the seduction hypothesis (p. 160). His discovery of the role of instinct and infantile sexuality changed both the understanding of phobias, as well as neurosis in general. No longer was the therapeutic goal one of uncovering the repressed memory with its associated affect, but rather one of uncovering the unconscious sexual fantasies which derived from instinct. The topographic model accounted for anxiety as a result of the failure of repression, and the therapeutic task made use of free association aimed at uncovering the repressed fantasies, thereby making the unconscious conscious.

The classic case of Little Hans's phobia (1909) demonstrates clinically the role of childhood sexuality in the creation of a phobia, as well as reconsidering the larger issue of how phobias should be classified.

Freud demonstrates through the use of a clinical report that "Hans really was a little Oedipus who wanted to have his father 'out of the way', to get rid of him, so that he might be alone with his beautiful mother and sleep with her" (p. 111). This death wish against his father was part of Hans's ambivalence toward a father whom he also deeply loved. This complex, and the conflicts to which it gave rise, led to Hans' horse phobia and provided a medium through which to further examine phobia formation.

Freud states that

> One day while Hans was in the street he was seized with an attack of anxiety. He could not yet say what it was he was afraid

> of; but at the very beginning of this anxiety-state he betrayed to his father his motive for being ill, the advantage he derived from it. He wanted to stay with his mother and to coax with her; his recollection that he had also been separated from her at the time of the baby's (i.e., his sister's) birth may also, as his father suggests, have contributed to his longing. It soon became evident that his anxiety was no longer reconvertible into longing, he was afraid even when his mother went with him. In the meantime indications appeared of what it was to which his libido (now changed into anxiety) had become attached. He gave expression to the quite specific fear that a white horse would bite him [pp. 114–115].

Freud described how Hans' sexual excitement was converted into anxiety and "assigned" a context, i.e., that a horse would bite him; how his oedipal wishes to be with his mother and his jealous and hostile wishes against his father led to his fear of his father and were transposed onto the horse.

Some of the pertinent issues, then, expressed in the Little Hans case are the concept of an Oedipus complex additionally influenced by the anal character of Hans's "lumpf" pregnancy fantasies, the way in which his oedipal neurosis was displaced into the horse phobia, the assumption that the phobia originated *from* the instinctual pressures of his oedipal desires and the fear of his father, and that this complex made use of the horse symbol. Freud also outlined the path of associations leading to the horse symbol and how they flowed from Hans seeing his friend Fritzl falling down while they were playing horses and "the fact that there was an easy path of association from Fritzl to his father" (pp. 136–137). While describing some of the other associative links to horses, Freud acknowledges that "even these connections would probably not have been sufficient if it had not been that, thanks to the pliability and ambiguity of associative chains, the same event showed itself capable of stirring the second of the complexes that lurked in Hans's unconscious, the complex of his pregnant mother's confinement. From that moment the way was clear for the return of the repressed; and it returned in such a manner that *the pathogenic material was remodelled and transposed on to the horse-complex, while the accompanying affects were uniformly turned into anxiety*" (p. 137)

Freud distinguished Hans's phobia from agoraphobia in that the agoraphobic patient is able to go out if he is accompanied by "some specially selected person." Since Hans's phobia did not improve, even when accompanied by his mother, it did not fulfill that condition.

In a statement that has strong implications for the consideration of phobias Freud appears to reverse his earlier position on distinct classicifation when he states, "In the classificatory system of the neuroses no definite position has hitherto been assigned to 'phobias.' It seems certain that they should only be regarded as syndromes which may form part of various neuroses and that we need not rank them as an independent pathological process" (p. 115). Freud here blurs the distinctions that a diagnosis of phobia would allow, he instead directs us to psychoanalytic theory as a whole.

He suggests (p. 115) that "anxiety-hysteria" would be an appropriate term for the kind of phobia to which Hans was subjected. Freud was struck by the similarity in this case to hysteria. In hysteric conversions, the libido was converted into a somatic innervation, whereas in Hans's phobia it was released in the form of anxiety. In obsessional disorders the libido was attached to an idea. We find, then, at this point in theory development, a "classificatory" system based on the transformations of libido.

Freud comments that "anxiety-hysterias are the most common of all psychoneurotic disorders." They are also among those which tend to occur earliest in development. He is still not clear ". . . whether anxiety-hysteria is determined, in contradistinction to conversion-hysteria and other neuroses, solely by constitutional factors or solely by accidental experiences, or by what combination of the two" (p. 116). He adds, however, that anxiety-hysteria is ". . . the least dependent upon a special constitutional predisposition and that it is consequently the most easily acquired at any time of life" (p. 116). He felt that "anxiety-hysteria tends to develop more and more into a phobia," (p. 116) and that the development of the phobia represents an attempt to bind the anxiety. "Nothing is left for it but to cut off access to every possible occasion that might lead to the development of anxiety, by erecting mental barriers in the nature of precautions, inhibitions, or prohibitions; and it is these defensive structures that appear to us in the form of phobias and that constitute to our eyes the essence of the disease" (p. 117).

The view of phobia current with the case of Little Hans is based on the theory of anxiety as transformed libido and the displaceability and binding of libido, for example, on to a phobic object. At this time the main criterion by which to assess mental phenomena was still based on its accessibility to consciousness. Therefore, the therapeutic task was one of making the unconscious conscious. What was unconscious of course was the repressed sexual wishes, wishes that persist into adulthood but were already demonstrable in the five-year-old boy.

The case reasserts the developmental model in psychoanalytic theory by demonstrating Hans's level of psychosexual development. Developmental models are so central to psychoanalytic theory that it is worth emphasizing this psychoanalytic assertion. Many modern theories differ from Freud's, or from one another, by positing alternative developmental models with specific phases of development. Some theorists may remain within the classical model of psychosexual development first proposed by Freud, but emphasize earlier levels of organization or the evolution of the ego. The understanding and analysis of a phobia will be determined in large part on the basis of the developmental model or emphasis by which the analyst organizes the clinical material. All analytic theories, however, conform to the necessity of a developmental point of view.

Another issue to be mentioned in considering phobia formation is the "choice" of phobic object. The instinctual basis of phobia is clear. External events such as the birth of Hans's sister had something to do with the development of his neurosis, but more insofar as it led to an increase in instinctual pressure. Freud implies at some points that the choice of phobic object is almost by chance, as when he describes (1909, p. 136) the "chance event" of seeing "the bus-horse fall down in the street." The neurosis makes use of a particular event. In the case of Little Hans, he was close to the station where horses came and went and, owing to this familiarity, the instinctual pressures and need for repression made use of this fact. At other times he suggests a somewhat more "deliberate" choice of phobic object, as when he describes how his father used to play horses with him. He refers to the compromise nature of the neurosis in that the fear of horses limits Little Hans' movement and freedom, but allows him to stay close to his beloved mother. Freud is aware, however, that any phobic object that was outside could have accomplished this same goal. Freud maintains that the phobic object is analogous to a manifest dream in that only the phobic's (dreamer's) associations will help to unravel the motive (latent content). Like the day residue of a dream, certain chance occurrence—like Fritzl falling down, or the proximity to horses in which Hans lived—may determine the phobic object, but the actual motive cause must still be looked for in the phobic's (dreamer's) instinctual life. The instincts take advantage of the opportunity to exert themselves through displacement onto the phobic object. Therefore one is not in a position to make statements about the nature of the instinct by noting the actual symptom, any more than one can make statements about the latent content of a dream without access to the dreamer's associations.

Freud also comments on the fact that when one first hears the description of a phobia it may not represent a complete picture of the neurosis. For example, the original description of Hans's phobia as a fear of horses became elaborated during the analysis to include carts and things that contained and unloaded objects, and so included the anal complex. The clinical relevance is that when a patient describes his phobia, further analytic investigation may reveal that it is not a "single" phobia. Other elements may be revealed, which both helps to clarify the underlying dynamics, and makes the phobia appear more complex than it might have seemed from its initial description.

The comparison to dreams is made in "Totem and Taboo" in connection with the concept of "systems." Freud here distinguishes between the instinctual causes of a neuroses (in Hans, for example, it was the oedipal neurosis) and calls this the "real" cause; and the secondary revision, which attempts to give sense to a neurosis, to try to make it look plausible. He compares this phenomenon to the secondary revision in a dream which tries to give the dream some kind of sense of cohesion, although there are obvious holes and inconsistencies in the manifest content of a dream. The ego tries to give the impression, as well, that the phobia makes sense. As with a dream, however, one cannot make causal sense of the phobia from its manifest content. One must apply the associative method, just as in the dream. Additionally, as one examines a phobia in more analytic detail, other features will emerge that make it clear that the phobia was not quite so consistent as it might have at first appeared. This is due to the need to create a system which is only partly successful at obscuring and disguising the underlying instinctual nature of the condition.

The case of the Wolf Man (1918) also describes a phobia in reconstructing the childhood of an obsessional neurotic adult. The outbreak of a childhood phobia followed on the occurrence of the now-famous wolf dream just before the patient's fourth birthday, and preceded the outbreak of an obsessional disorder at the age of four-and-a-half. Freud sums up the phobic element quite nicely (1918, p. 112) as he asks us to

> now consider the phobia. It came into existence on the level of the genital organization, and shows us the relatively simple mechanism of an anxiety-hysteria. The ego, by developing anxiety, was protecting itself against what it regarded as an overwhelming danger, namely, homosexual satisfaction. But the process of repression left behind it a trace which cannot be

> overlooked. The object to which the dangerous sexual aim had been attached had to have its place taken in consciousness by another one. What became conscious was fear not of the *father* but of the *wolf*. Nor did the process stop at the formation of a phobia with a single content. A considerable time afterwards the wolf was replaced by the lion.

A butterfly phobia also occurred and revealed the same psychical mechanism that was represented by the wolf phobia. Freud continues

> It may truly be said that the anxiety that was concerned in the formation of these phobias was a fear of castration. This statement involves no contradiction of the view that the anxiety originated from the repression of homosexual libido. Both modes of expression refer to the same process: namely, the withdrawal of libido by the ego from the homosexual wishful impulses, the libido having then become converted into free anxiety and subsequently bound in phobia [pp. 112–113].

Freud further argues that this was a case of true hysteria by offering additional evidence that the patient suffered a hysteric conversion symptom in that "his bowel behaved like a hysterically affected organ. The unconscious repressed homosexuality withdrew into his bowel" (p. 113).

The neurotic process was later transformed into an obsessional disorder. "The sadistic-masochistic sexual organization came slowly to an end, the wolf phobia quickly vanished, and, instead of sexuality being repudiated with anxiety, a higher method of suppressing it made its appearance. Piety became the dominant force in the child's life. These victories, however, were not won without struggles, of which his blasphemous thoughts were an indication, and of which the establishment of an obsessive exaggeration of religious ceremonial was the result" (p. 114).

Some important elements in this case were the description of the negative Oedipus complex, as contrasted to the positive Oedipus of Little Hans, but that the mechanism of phobia formation was the same in that repression led to anxiety, which was bound by displacement onto the phobic object. The case also describes the intimate nature of the relationship between phobia (anxiety-hysteria), conversion hysteria, and obsessional disorder. The theoretical framework at this point was still one of anxiety resulting from the failure of repression.

In "Repression" (1915a), Freud directs his attention to the formation of substitutes.

> "The mechanism of a repression becomes accessible to us only by our deducing that mechanism from the *outcome* of the repression. Confining our observations to the effect of repression on the ideational portion of the representative, we discover that as a rule it creates a *substitutive formation*.
>
> "The formation of the substitute for the ideational portion [of the instinctual representative] has come about by *displacement* along a chain of connections which is determined in a particular way. The quantitative potion has not vanished, but has been transformed into anxiety. The result is fear of a wolf, instead of a demand for love from the father." [pp. 154–155].

In "The Unconscious" (1915b) Freud refers to three "phases" of phobia formation. "In anxiety hysteria a first phase of the process is frequently overlooked, and may perhaps be in fact missed out; on careful observation, however, it can be clearly discerned. It consists in anxiety appearing without the subject knowing what he is afraid of" (p. 182). Working with the libido theory, Freud explains this as a result of an unconscious libidinal impulse seeking discharge through connection with preconscious ideation. The preconscious cathexis is rejected, however, and so the unconscious libidinal impulse is released in the form of anxiety.

In the second phase of the process some attempt at mastering a repetition of this anxiety is made. "The [*Pcs.*] cathexis that has taken flight attaches itself to a substitutive idea which, on the one hand, is connected by association with the rejected idea, and, on the other, has escaped repression by reason of its remoteness from that idea" (p. 182). This is a metapsychological description of the evolving displacement and represents a compromise of representation and disguise. It moderates the anxiety through the expression of some related, less disturbing ideational content, even though the idea is now a substitute for the original representative of the unconscious instinctual object. This substitute also "plays the part of an anticathexis for the system *Cs.* (*Pcs.*) by securing it against an emergence in the *Cs.* of the repressed idea" (p. 182). In other words, the creation of a substitute idea allows both the expression and an opportunity for the repression of the unacceptable impulse, and helps to prevent the original unacceptable idea from emerging into conscious awareness. "On the other hand it is, or acts as if it were, the point of departure for the release of the anxiety-affect, which has now really become quite uninhibitable" (p. 182). Anxiety is then generated by either of two situations: either an increase in the instinctual impulse or the presentation of the phobic situation. "The substitutive idea acts in the one instance as a point at which there is a passage across from the system *Ucs.* to the system *Cs.*, and, in the other instance, as a self-sufficing source for the release of anxiety" (p. 182). As the system *Cs.* dominates, the generation of anxiety tends to be more and more produced by the phobic situation, until the unconscious roots are almost completely inapparent. It is only in the phobic's inaccessibility to influence that the unconscious instinctual roots are revealed. The substitution through displacement represents the second phase of phobia formation. The third phase consists of attempts to avoid the generation of anxiety from the substitute, the phobic object. This involves a hypercathexis of the "associated environment of the substitutive idea" so that any related perception will arouse a small degree of anxiety. This anxiety provides a "signal to inhibit, by means of a fresh flight on the part of the [*Pcs.*] cathexis, the further progress of the development of anxiety" (p. 183). We see here the beginnings of the signal concept of anxiety.

The precautions that the phobia and its associated environment of stimuli make use of can only protect against "excitations which approach the substitutive idea from outside, through perception; they never guard against instinctual excitation, which reaches the substitutive idea from the direction of its link with the repressed idea" (p. 183). Therefore, the precautions work best when they have "taken over" most completely as representatives of the repressed, but they are always at risk from increased instinctual pressure. If instinctual pressure does increase, there is often a need to *extend* the phobic environment in a further attempt at protection. "The flight from a conscious cathexis of the substitutive idea is manifested in the avoidances, renunciations and prohibitions by which we recognize anxiety hysteria" (pp. 183–184). The third phase in phobia formation is analogous to the second phase. In the third phase, the system *Cs.* protects itself from the substitute idea (also in the system *Cs.*) by an anticathexis of the environment, while in the second phase the system *Cs.* protects itself from the repressed (in the system *Ucs.*) through an anticathexis of the substitute idea. Both represent forms of substitution through displacement (one from *Ucs.* – *Cs,* the other from *Cs.* – *Cs.*). The whole mechanism makes for a projection of the danger so that the danger is perceived of as coming from outside rather than from the internal, instinctual pressure.

While there are no direct references to phobias in "The Ego and the Id" (1923), its crucial position in the evolution of psychoanalytic thought deserves to be emphasized. The third phase of psychoanalytic theory begins here and allowed for insights on the nature of signal anxiety and the defensive functions of the ego in phobias. It also led to another shift in Freud's understanding of agoraphobia and its final classification among the psychoneuroses. Free association continued as the clinical method, but the therapeutic focus shifted to one of expanding the ego's control over the id.

In "Inhibitions, Symptoms and Anxiety" (1926) Freud undertakes a major reconsideration of anxiety. Because phobias are so closely associated with anxiety, the work becomes a major reexamination of the cases of Little Hans and the Wolf Man.

The question recurs of how to consider the essence of phobia. Is it an inhibition or a symptom, and how are these to be related to the anxiety readily apparent in phobias? Freud describes how in Little Hans case his "fear of horses was the symptom and his inability to go out into the streets was an inhibition, a restriction which his ego had imposed on itself so as not to arouse the anxiety symptom" (p. 101). He clarifies, however, that Hans suffered from a more specific fear, that a horse would bite him, and that the phobia of horses obscured to some degree this more specific fear.

Hans's phobia was an attempt to solve an oedipal conflict, and the repression of his hostile impulses toward his father. Hans was not consciously aware of the fear of his father's retaliation. He replaced the fear of his father with the fear that a horse would bite him and here, *displacement* is an essential element in the phobic symptom, essential because if Hans, for example, were afraid that his father would retaliate for Hans's hostile wishes it would not be considered a phobia. "The conflict is dealt with by one of the ambivalent feelings being directed to a substitute" (1926, p. 103). The substitution in children of animals for people is made easier by their tendency to less readily distinguish between humans and animals. Notice, however, that the displacement was not simply of his hostile, murderous impulses, or else Hans might simply have wished to see horses fall down, or to beat them, and this was clearly not the central feature of his phobia. Even if he had wished to see horses mistreated it would still not deserve the designation of a phobia. This would have been an alteration in the object of his hostile impulses, but not of the impulse itself. Something happened to the nature of the instinct as well in the formation of the phobia.

The case of the Wolf Man also reveals the substitution of an animal, the wolf, for the father. In the Wolf Man, however, "the idea of being devoured by the father gives expression, in a form that has undergone regressive degradation, to a passive, tender impulse to be loved by him in a genital-erotic sense" (1926, p. 105). The impulse expresses itself in "the language belonging to the superseded transitional phase between the oral and sadistic organization of the libido." It is a regressive form of the impulse. "At any rate, we can see that repression is not the only means which the ego can employ for the purpose of defence against an unwelcome instinctual impulse. If it succeeds in making an instinct regress, it will actually have done it more injury than it could have by repressing it. Sometimes, indeed, after forcing an instinct to regress in this way, it goes on to repress it" (p. 105). Thus displacement and regression are both processes implicated in the examination of phobias.

In both cases hostile impulses against the father were repressed. The Wolf Man phobia also had to contend with erotic impulses toward the father, which underwent regression and repression. In the case of Little Hans, the phobia had the "effect of abolishing his affectionate object-cathexis of his mother, though the actual content of his phobia betrayed no sign of this" (p. 106). In both cases, the phobia attempted to solve the oedipal struggles, in the Wolf Man the negative Oedipus and in Little Hans the positive Oedipus. How to account for the fact that these cases, one of the positive, the other of the negative Oedpus, both led to phobia formation? Freud answers, "This motive force was the same in both of them. It was the fear of impending castration" (pp. 107–108). Hans's aggressiveness led to his fear of castration in retaliation and was displaced to the fear that a horse would bite his genitals. The Wolf Man's passive desires led to the fear that that would require castration. Both forms of the Oedipus led to the fear of castration.

Freud next considers the element of anxiety, which is also central to the question of phobias and formally alters his position that anxiety results from repression through transformed libido. He rather asserts that anxiety was the motive for repression. "The anxiety belonging to the animal phobias was an untransformed fear of castration." Freud adds, "It was therefore a realistic fear, a fear of a danger which was actually impending or was judged to be a real one" (1926, p. 108). Signal anxiety is now understood as an attempt at avoiding traumatic anxiety.

Freud states (p. 109), "The anxiety felt in animal phobias is the ego's fear of castration; while the anxiety felt in agoraphobia . . . seems to be its fear of sexual temptation—a fear which, after all, must be connected in its origins with the fear of castration." He proceeds: "As far as can be seen at present, the majority of phobias go back to an anxiety of this kind felt by the ego in regard to the demands of the libido."

Freud initially states that the fear of castration is the ultimate motive force for phobias. He later mitigates this claim by stating that the "majority" of phobias are to be regarded in this way. Precisely which phobias are to be excluded from this claim is not clarified. There is still some uncertainty (expressed on p. 110) on the nature of anxiety neurosis as to whether anxiety may be caused by disturbed sexual practices. Perhaps he is not yet ready to conclude that agoraphobia fits in completely with the dynamics he describes here. It is not until 1933 that Freud finally recants accumulated libido as the cause of anxiety in anxiety neurosis, when he states "we shall no longer maintain that it is the libido itself that is turned into anxiety in such cases" (p. 94).

Freud (1926) asserts that the motive cause for phobias, as well as conversion hysteria and obsessional neurosis, is the fear of castration and the handling of the Oedipus complex. The strength of this position is diluted by the expression of doubt about the invariable role of the fear of castration, and (on p. 143) he considers the possibility that in hysteria in women it may be rather the fear of loss of the object's love that is central among the potential dangers. He further deemphasizes the inevitable role of the castration threat in young children when he states in regard to the "phobias of early childhood . . . such as the fear of being alone or in the dark or with strangers . . ." that these are "reactions to the danger of losing the object" (p. 168). Still others "like the fear of small animals, thunderstorms, etc., might perhaps be accounted for as vestigial traces of the congenital preparedness to meet real dangers which is so strongly developed in other animals" (p. 168).

"Inhibitions, Symptoms and Anxiety" contains the last revisions on the subject of phobias. Except for very brief mention in "Moses and Monotheism" (1939), Freud's final writing on the subject occurs in the "New Introductory Lectures" (1933) in Lecture XXXII and contains nothing new.

Freud's varying positions on the subject of phobias actually provides an opportunity to consider the disorder from a number of perspectives in a manner similar to attempts to understand the place of each of Freud's models (e.g., reflect arc, topographic, and structural). (Gedo & Goldberg, 1973). The construction and choice of models in psychoanalytic work risks the possible defensive use of one model (Spira, 1988) but also provides the potential for a valuable integration.

It has been demonstrated that Freud struggled with the problem of how best to understand phobias, especially agoraphobia, and one gets the impression in reviewing his work that he was never quite satisfied with his understanding of this disorder. Freud's difficulty is reflected in the modern debates over the nature of agoraphobia and suggests the possibility that it might be more useful to conceptualize two distinct disorders. One class of phobia corresponds to Freud's view of agoraphobia as an actual neurosis, and the other class is best conceptualized by his structural theory of psychoneurosis.

The view expressed in his discussion of actual neurosis is that anxiety is primary, i.e., it has a somatic origin, and only secondarily attaches to ideas suited to become the object of a phobia. The patient hopes to avoid another attack of anxiety by avoiding the phobic situation. It is an attempt at mastery and limiting the anticipatory anxiety.

Such a patient, however, may also have significant, coexisting psychological conflicts, and the anxiety generated somatically may attach to those *conflicts*. The patient in this situation will not appreciate that his anxiety represents a somatic disorder. He will rather attribute it, consciously or unconsciously, to those psychological conflicts which are central.

For example, a patient for whom separation issues are most significant will attribute the "cause" of an anxiety attack, even if it has a somatic origin, to issues related to separation. This may give the clinician the impression of a particularly powerful psychoneurosis that is resistant to interpretive work. Even if the somatic anxiety were to resolve it will have left it's mark, perhaps in more persistent or extensive defensive operations on the part of the ego.

I am not attempting to engage the larger question of the relation of actual neuroses and psychoneuroses, but rather to demonstrate that Freud's varying views may actually allow of an integration that will enhance the understanding of each position.

REFERENCES

Breuer, J. & Freud, S. (1893–1895). Studies on hysteria. *S.E.*, 2.

Freud, S. (1893). On the psychical mechanism of hysterical phenomena. *S.E.*, 3.

_____ (1894). The neuro-psychoses of defence. *S.E.*, 3.

_____ (1895). Obsessions and phobias: Their psychical mechanism and their aetiology. *S.E.*, 3.

_____ (1905). Three essays on the theory of sexuality. *S.E.*, 7.

_____ (1909). Analysis of a phobia in a five-year-old boy. *S.E.*, 10.

_____ (1913). Totem and taboo. *S.E.*, 13.

_____ (1915a). The unconscious. *S.E.*, 14.

_____ (1915b). Repression. *S.E.*, 14.

_____ (1918). From the history of an infantile neurosis. *S.E.*, 17.

_____ (1923). The ego and the id. *S.E.*, 19.

_____ (1926). Inhibitions, symptoms and anxiety. *S.E.*, 20.

_____ (1933). New introductory lectures on psycho-analysis. Lecture XXXII: Anxiety and Instinctual Life. *S.E.*, 22.

_____ (1939). Moses and monotheism. *S.E.*, 23.

Gedo, J. & Goldberg, A. (1973). *Models of the Mind.* Chicago: Univ. Chicago Press.

Spira, D. (1988). The defensive function of psychoanalytic theories. *Annual Psychoanal.*, 16:81–92.

Strachey, J. (1962). Freud's views on phobias. Appendix to Freud's Obsessions and phobias. *S.E.*, 3.

180 N. Michigan Avenue
Chicago, IL 60601

Fear, Phobia, and Panic

JOSEPH D. LICHTENBERG, M.D.

ANYONE FAMILIAR WITH THE EXTENSIVE literature on fear (anxiety), phobias, and panic disorders is inevitably impressed by the complexity of the topic. One set of questions can be formed from within the traditional structural hypothesis (Spira). Is anxiety to be singled out as a special response pattern, which, as a signal, is central to the function of the psychic apparatus? Are phobias one of a group of psychoneuroses susceptible to straightforward analysis of the conflicts, compromise formations, and symbolic meanings by classical psychoanalytic techniques? Are panic disorders the result of the failure of the ego to restrict anxiety to its signal function or to the failure to create a stable symptom (compromise formation) such as a phobia through symbolic representations and defensive activity? Another set of questions can derive from alternative perspectives cited or implied by one or more of our contributors. Is fear one of a group of basic affects, each having great psychological significance but none having special intrapsychic adaptational importance? An affirmative answer to this proposal brings into question the psychoanalytic tradition of distinguishing between fear and anxiety and assigning signal anxiety a central functional role. How are we to regard empirical data that indicates unusual difficulty in the analysis of many phobic patients? Are we failing to ascribe sufficient significance to residues of traumatization (Rocah)? Are

Dr. Lichtenberg is Editor-in-Chief of *Psychoanalytic Inquiry* and a member of the Faculty of the Washington Psychoanalytic Institute.

we not recognizing the core dynamic problem to be fear of humiliation (Gedo) or fear of novelty (Moraitis)? What is the relationship of phobias to panic disorders? Are phobias defenses against panic disorders? Are panic disorders failed phobias or separate entities? Are panic disorders more biological than psychodynamic in origin (Busch et al.)? Or are panic disorders cognitive states of misidentification of physical risk (Busch et al.)—or reexperienced trauma (Rocah)?

Fear

The earliest recognizable manifestation of fear is the neonate's response pattern when startled. The response when overwhelmingly intense takes the form of a Moro reflex with a jolting back and rigidity of all body parts. The more common response is jerkiness, startle, followed by crying. If small infants are in contact with their mother when startled they will tighten their grip on a body part, an automatic gesture of seeking security. Grip tightening may be the innate link between fear and seeking security through dependence, cited by Busch et al.

Fear in adults is a clearly recognizable distinct affect with a characteristic facial expression of eyes widening, mouth opening, head and body tensing and retracting, heart and breathing rates quickening, blood pressure increasing, and other autonomic nervous responses. The facial and bodily characteristics of fear are clearly recognizable in infants by eight months (Emde, 1983) and, in the view of others, earlier (Demos, 1985) especially when abusive treatment has occurred (Fraiberg, 1982; Gaensbauer, 1982). I regard fear as one of a group of affects of an aversive motivational system. This system self-organizes and self-stabilizes in response to the need to react with antagonism and/or withdrawal to stimuli experienced as aversive. The smallest infant can cry, push out a nipple, tense the body, and turn the head away. From these general manifestations of distress that have the fight-flight qualities cited by ethologists, parents rather quickly discern specific affects. Angry crying, angry rejecting and disgust or distaste are early indicators of differentiating forms of antagonism. Fear crying, fearful avoidance, whole body freezing, low keyedness or sadness, and the drooping face and body of shame are early indicators of differentiating forms of withdrawal. A dialectic tension exists within the system as to what form the aversive response will take. For example, Fraiberg (1982) cites an extremely combative 13-month-old raised in an abusive environment whose facial expression showed a flicker of fear before his self-exhaustive antagonistic outbursts. The facial tics, especially those around his eyes, of a patient of mine originated in his blinking and flinching as a toddler when hit by his father, a procedural memory (see Lichtenberg, 1989) response his treatment helped him to anticipate and resist with his son. Comparable perceptual stimuli such as a parent's threatening frown may lead some children primarily to anger, others to fear, still others to a combination—sometimes with sadness or shame included. The findings of the multiplicity of responses in infants coincides with a multiplicity of affects connected with fear, phobia, and panic disorders in the adult cases reported by our contributors.

To regard fear as an inborn response to perceived danger is a formulation so grounded in ethology that we can easily fail to consider what it means for the human. The only vestige of direct threat of the predator in human infants may be the automatic aversive response to a looming head (Beebe & Stern, 1977). Infants are remarkably ill prepared innately to perceive danger. Infants and older children will respond to hunger and thirst by imbiding foods, medicines, and fluids that will make them sick. Their needs for attachment experiences and even moments of intimacy pleasure will lead them to shadow, seek out, and submissively engage with parents who for the most part cause them pain and disappointment. Their avidity for exploration and assertion will lead them to follow a ball out into a dangerous street, climb up an unstable support, or put fingers in electric plugs. Their love of sensual enjoyment from fondling, kissing, and rocking will result in their participating in sexually overexciting play or overt seductions with older children and adults. The pleasure of social contact will expose older children to the smiling-faced inducements of a kidnapper, and the same desire coupled with greed leaves adults exposed to the psychopathic salesman and conman. Thus parents must inculcate a sense of danger as an active educative effort.

Two factors work together to produce an internal sense of danger. First, infants are amazingly perceptive trackers of contingency and, second, caregivers must of necessity prohibit and warn children about the manifold dangers of everyday life—don't touch, hot, not in your mouth, careful you'll fall, take my hand. Consequently with very few exceptions danger is an experience a child learns to anticipate—whether it is the danger of actually falling from a ladder or the danger of being shouted at and punished for climbing the forbidden ladder. The nature of the experience changes with development—at first infants reach for an object and their parents stop them, saying No! No!, then older infants to toddlers start to reach and hold back the gesture maybe themselves saying No, and later the whole sequence can be carried out in thought without gesture.

I believe the traditional distinction between fear as an automatic response, anxiety as anticipated danger, and signal anxiety as the special capacity without which the ego would be powerless to control overwhelming drive, is of limited value. The "automatic" response to the looming head or to startle is far too limited a base for a conception of fear. Very quickly all fear experiences become anticipatory—whether fear of the unexpected (novelty [Moraitis] and startle) or of a known danger and its traumatic effect (Rocah). Should signal anxiety retain the privileged position in our theory that Freud gave it? Brenner (1975, 1976) has already suggested it should be shared with signal depression—the negative response to a danger assumed to have already occurred and other intensely unpleasurable affects. Self psychologists emphasize signal shame, embarrassment, or humiliation—if I fail at this test I will feel ashamed of myself, or embarrassed or humiliated in front of others. I believe we are led into these dilemmas about signal anxiety by a linguistic looseness, we say *fear* when we mean *anticipation.* Anticipation is inherent in Freud's conception of thought as trial action. If I am about to go to a movie rather than study, I may anticipate the consequent failure on a test and sample the shame or embarrassment or humiliation I will suffer, and I may inhibit the recreational motive. We might call this *fear* of shame, but I would not necessarily *experience* fear. Another example is "fear of success" by which we mean: if I succeed at this task I will outdo my parent and I will feel guilty. Guilt is the anticipated affect that calls for inhibiting the motive of competence and acquisitiveness. Guilt, not fear, is the anticipated experience, and outdoing a rival toward whom one feels indebted, not success, is the danger that triggers the guilt. An analyst summarizing an hour might say it was dominated by the patient's castration anxiety. This might refer to a generalized anxiousness or fearfulness the patient was experiencing, or to the expression of diffuse or highly specific bodily concerns, or to the description of a rival's physical size or mental prowess without any experienced fear.

If fear is a particular affective experience triggered by an encounter with the unfamiliar or a reencounter with a known danger, what are the means by which its intensity is regulated? This is how Katie at four months was dunked for the first time in a swimming pool. When held at arm's length and slowly but playfully exposed to the water, she looked startled and cried. When her mother held her close to her body, Katie calmed, and then her mother, holding Katie against her, dunked the two in the water. Katie was now delighted by the experience. The physical presence of another, the body to touch, the hand to hold, and later its symbolic equivalent in the transitional object, and still later the memento, becomes established as a means to control fear. I suggest one means by which touching or being "in touch with" a loving other counters fear is by providing a reminder of the familiar as an antidote to a total preoccupation with the novel or the dangerous.

Let us apply this hypothesis to the "stranger anxiety" of the nine-month-old. Infants of this age will suddenly become frightened in the presence of nonhousehold members toward whom they previously would have shown interest. However, the experimental setting exerts a strong influence on the outcome. If infants are in an unfamiliar setting, say, a crib in a laboratory, and a stranger enters, the fear response will be elicited consistently. If infants are observed at home in their cribs with mother standing by or in mother's lap, the stranger's entry may elicit interest with or without wariness. The entry of the relatively familiar grandmother or the totally unknown visiting aunt does not itself determine the response. The response is determined by the presence of the mother's security providing support, measured against other factors, such as the startle pressure exerted by the mode of the stranger's entry—rapid and intense or slow and friendly. This explanation is accurate but incomplete in that it fails to recognize that infants at nine months utilize a different means to elicit a sense of security in the presence of novelty. Katie at four months received her sense of security from sensing her mother's physical self by touch, sight, smell, and sound; nine-month-olds read the affective state of their mother by rapidly scanning her facial expression. Mother's smile conveys the information I am pleased or this person is our friend; mother's frown indicates I am displeasured or this person's presence arouses annoyance; mother's fear expression means I am frightened or this person's presence arouses alarm. From this time on infants are guided by the subjective interplay of the emotions of others and of themselves. But as yet they are practiced at "reading" the affective facial expressions of only those most familiar to them. Following this line of reasoning, the "stranger," who often is not at all an unknown person, is one whose affect state cannot be read and whose friendly intent cannot be instantly incorporated into the infant's security system.

Infants at about nine months are thus between two markedly different methods of processing information. An aversive state of wary or fearful avoidance of people who previously were a source of interested exploration results from the dialectic tension between an old approach that provided security and a new maturational advance not yet absorbed adequately into the infant's repertoire. The almost universal inclination toward distrust of the stranger-foreigner (such as the presumably "inscrutable Oriental") whose affect state we cannot easily assess suggests that this dialectic tension may never be fully resolved.

This reanalysis of stranger anxiety allows us to recognize that the regulation of fear arises from two sources, one interpersonal, one intrapsychic. The interpersonal derives from a sense of being supported, existing in an empathic ambience of caring, competently protective people. The intrapsychic derives from a sense of being able to physically and cognitively recognize and avail oneself of the security potential in the environment. The capacity to recognize and avail oneself of security requires the ability to temper the enticing excitement of the novel with establishing the familiar. Establishing a sense of the familiar can be accomplished by action patterns (the touching of the infant), affect referencing (facial scanning of the young toddler), or by symbolic referencing (conjuring up mother's image or recognizing some familiar elements among the unfamiliar by the three-year-old). Throughout life older children and adults have available all three means of regulating fear.

Phobias

Moraitis draws on my compilation of the evidence for a distinct motivational system built around the innate human need to explore and assert preferences (Lichtenberg, 1989). Free of the need for physiological requirements, uninvolved with attachment activities, infants will explore their surroundings with interest, pursue whatever goals their preferences establish (such as getting their fingers in their mouth or eye-scanning a mobile), and work to activate a sense of increasing efficiency and competence. As Moraitis notes, the intense human need and desire to turn the world into a realm of self-selected knowledge leads to confrontations with the novel and the potentiality for triggering fear, but when successful, reduces the novel to the familiar through understanding, thus triggering an increasing sense of security. Moraitis believes that many phobias are the result of patients' failed efforts to confront the novel. In these instances processing information is derailed, the sense of security from reducing the novel to the familiar through understanding is not achieved. Instead, following Gedo, we can assume the person feels humiliated rather than effective and proud. And following Rocah, were helplessness and humiliation to continue, the person would experience a traumatic state. Following Meissner, the person would activate an innately present potential for aggression as an attempt to overcome the obstacles of helplessness and humiliation and to emerge from the traumatic state. At this point, following Freud and all our contributors, the person may unconsciously construct a phobia, which serves as a compromise formation for the intrapsychic tension or conflictual state. An external object or situation is selected as the presumed source of danger because it symbolically represents the unconscious conflicted contents (fantasy or belief system). Meyer and Maletic emphasize that the complete phobic syndrome includes not only avoidance of a feared object but a strong interest and attachment to it.

I would add that not only is the feared object a source of interest and attachment but that, in the phobic patient's history, fear itself may have been sought for. We recognize the usual interactive tension between fear and safety as aiming toward the latter. Fear, however, (like any strong affect) may be invigorating—as evidenced by amusement park rides and horror movies. For some patients, fear may have been sought for its vitalizing potential before the illness occurs. We often refer to this behavior as counterphobic, emphasizing its defensive quality, and fail to recognize the draw such invigorating affects have, especially for people otherwise devoid of animation.

The fate of the phobia, once formed, is variable. The phobia may be transitory, as in the common brief zoophobias of childhood. After the birth of her sister, a four-year-old became intensely upset and insomniac. She said she was terrified at seeing bugs and was afraid to sleep lest she see (dream of?) thousands of bugs. After much comfort and reassurance plus sexual enlightenment the symptom disappeared without known impact 25 years later.

The phobia may be a persistent but circumscribed symptom that may be resolved when subjected to analysis. Examples are the elevator phobia of Moraitis's patient and the agoraphobia of Meissner's patient. In these cases the patient may present any variety of personality type or other psychopathological formations. I believe phobias of this circumscribed type tell the story of a specific conflict within the larger story of the patient's whole life. The story told in Moraitis's Ms. A's elevator phobia was: I want to explore a new experience of intimacy with a man—my fiancee, you—but I am afraid of losing my sense of independence and becoming devalued like my phobic mother. I can't come to you because I can't use the elevator. Parenthetically, the symbolism of elevator as rising sexual excitement, were it to have been found in Ms. A's associations, would have provided additional specificity to her condensed narrative. In Meissner's patient, the agoraphobia allowed her to outdo her sister's claims on their mother's concern and attention. She was saying: I'm needy like my sisters, so favor me as you did them; I'm not angry at you but a phobic victim just like you. Gedo's patient's fear of drowning echoed his early "fears of succumbing to the pull for symbolic fusion with an enormously seductive, intrusive, egocentric, and infantile mother." Gedo notes that the core analog to the story articulated in the phobia lay not in the abstract symbol of the engulfing mother, but in the putative sensation of drowning, which provided a condensed affective *sensation* of the mother-child relationship—"being close to my mother is like helplessly drowning in her craziness."

In evaluating the formation of his patient's fear of drowning, Gedo states, "the phobia, established because of the unmanageable anxieties stirred up by the Phyrric victory of the oedipal child, was operative in a segment of mental life seemingly structured in a manner expectable in Mode IV." Gedo's patient's phobia would be similar to that of Little Hans, a formation of the oedipal phase, while other of the patient's symptoms were organized according to the modes of earlier functioning. Gedo follows both our traditional hierarchical conceptualizing and the logic that indicates that complex organizations develop slowly. Further support for the oedipal-period mode of processing information comes from the common occurrence of animal and other phobias during this time. This epoch is a time when children are actively composing narratives about who they are (Stern, 1985), and are often flooded with information and feeling states too new and puzzling to integrate.

But our ordinary timetable is confounded by such clinical findings as the well-documented case of a phobia in an 18-month-old (Renik et al., 1978). This toddler refused suddenly to play in his back yard, explaining he was afraid of "dangerous bamboo." This precocious youngster, spurred on by his mother, was well aware of sexual activity such as coitus, the names and appearance of his, his sister's, and parent's genitals. He was openly jealous of his parent's attentions to each other and attacked his father's genitals. In his treatment, he revealed that observing his father's hammering and sawing triggered a fantasy that his penis might be cut by an owl hiding in the bamboo or by a sharp stick of bamboo. The dangerous owl lurking in the branches and the broken stalk were connected with his image of a damaged female genital hidden in a thicket of pubic hair. He also believed that his penis, like his feces, might fall off into the toilet, resulting in an aversion to flushing.

What does this report tell us about the degree of psychic organization necessary to form a phobia? I believe it indicates that phobias can occur beginning at 15 months when the capacity for symbolic representation in the dual modes of primary and secondary process is operant as a result of the maturation (myelinization) of the frontal cortex and associational paths in both hemispheres. The possibility of a phobia being formed at this early age is less surpising when we consider this is the age when dreaming also begins and that dream mentation and the mentation of phobic formation are basically similar.

Most of our contributors point out that in one way or another phobias serve adaptation as well as being pathologic. I would like to discuss the adaptational side, using three examples of phobias developed by patients during the course of analysis.

Mr. A had desperate longings to share his life with a woman but was only able to achieve orgasm homosexually. At a critical point in his analysis he stated his intent to buy a home in a homosexual neighborhood. I told him that to do so was to preclude the opportunity to analyze the intense fears of closeness with women that his dating was triggering. He agreed and instead moved into an apartment inhabited by heterosexual couples. He suddenly developed intense nocturnal claustrophiba, running out of his apartment into the streets. Analysis revealed the trigger was his hearing sounds from other apartments which he interpreted as coitus and which flooded him with primal scene memories from childhood. The analysis of these memory-fantasies and associated beliefs of the female's engulfing powers were the turning points in his successful quest for a heterosexual solution.

Mrs. B entered analysis with a cancer phobia and numerous inhibitions. The long, difficult opening and middle phases of her analysis were marked by several restrictions she placed on self-revelation characterized by prolonged silences. As the tenor of the working ambience between us gradually improved with her increased tolerance of her own barely contained rage, she expressed a wish to have a baby and shortly thereafter revealed a pregnancy phobia. The pregnancy phobia served as a barrier to a goal she intensely desired and simultaneously provided a much needed motive to use analysis to rid herself of this obstacle. The tenor of the work changed with relevant associations, allowing us to connect her wishes, past events and fantasies, and transference fears to the pregnancy phobia. She underwent a successful pregnancy and then opened the way to links to her cancer phobia, which required considerably more analytic work.

Ms. C entered analysis with numerous complaints. She felt she had reason to believe she was unusually bright but had failed to accomplish much. She attached herself to a series of men she regarded as powerful only to become disappointed with each. More than any other patient I have worked with she resolutely refused to consider any direct or indirect reference to me, our interactions, or transference associations. If I pressed her about it she fell asleep and generally missed the next hour while denying any connections. I understood her to have established a preanalytic idealized transference which she was desperate to preserve. With minimal extratransference interpretations on my part, she gradually made many changes in her life. She broke with her old lover, recognized the destructiveness of her promiscuity, and made a stable marriage. Most important to her, after years of embarrassing postponements she completed the requirements for her Ph.D. brilliantly. She frequently had near-panic attacks when she put her daughter by a previous marriage on a plane to visit the child's father. We understood this as a response to her guilt about times she had shunted the child off to carry on one of her affairs. After acquiring her Ph.D., Ms. C's work changed, requiring her to make frequent flights. She developed an airplane phobia that threatened her career. This threat provided the motivation necessary for me to persuade her to relax her obstinate avoidance of using the analytic experience as a source of understanding. The fantasy she revealed as we worked back and forth between airplane and analytic situation was that in the plane she was helpless to use her brain to guide the plane, while in the cockpit were pilot and copilot incompetent and indifferent to the safety of the passengers. She recovered childhood memories of terror at the sound of screeching brakes and ambulance sirens, based on her expectation that one of her numerous poorly tended siblings was being hit by a car. We connected her childhood terror to her present fears of the airplane and of discovering or confirming my incompetence. Subsequently, the rate and depth of the analytic work proceeded to a successful termination.

What can we conclude from these examples of analyzable and resolvable discrete phobias? Before the phobia was created my patients were in a state of diffuse tension similar to that reported in Little Hans (Freud, 1909) and the child with the bamboo phobia. I regard my patients as having been wrestling with information stirred in the analysis, and Hans and the bamboo panic with information stirred largely by stimuli in their external environment. They were propelled to explore information they were simultaneously propelled to avoid, and their inner resources were unable to resolve this dialectic tension. The analyst as coexplorer gave impetus to the side of the conflict involving tackling the novelty, while as transference figure representing a source of aversive need the analyst gave impetus to an anxious avoidance. The patient creates a solution—pull the information together into a coherent story, put the story in a form the self can't read and so can avoid, but have a story that a safety-providing other can read and thus help to resolve. The last part of this formulation—having a story that a safety providing other can read and thus help to resolve—may be creditable for a phobia that forms during the course of an analysis, but how can it apply to other phobias? I draw support from the analogous situation that mankind has from time immemorial formed dreams and symptoms that are integrated stories unknowable to the creator but told to another in hopes of decoding. Pharaoh tells his dreams to Joseph. And all cultures provide for this human pattern by providing a special professional class of Shaman, priest, Rabbi, exorcist, and others presumed to serve as oracles capable of revealing hidden meanings. Stated another way, society responds to the interplay between fear triggered by novelty and danger and security triggered by familiarity and a safe haven, by providing safety via wise men capable of translating the too novel into the controllably familiar. I draw additional support for my thesis that the phobia provides a story that a safety-producing other can read from the observational that this involving another succeeds not only in analysis but in ordinary life as well. Most childhood zoophobias as well as many brief fear-avoidance states at any time in life "disappear." On closer examination the frightened child, like the little girl with the bug phobia, alert their parents to their state. The parents may not know how to decode the "story" of the conflicting forces involved in the informational overload, but they intuitively are drawn into getting involved: "Don't be frightened, we won't let any harm come to you. There are no tigers here. Tigers aren't allowed to bite people. They are kept in cages at the zoo. If we go to the zoo we won't go near the tiger's cage, or if we do I'll hold your hand very tight." And they often add an intuitive interpretation—"I bet you're upset because mommy had to be away or because you were punished for hitting your little brother." Thus parents often devise some means of both approximating the encoded message and designing a mini behavior-modification program. At the least they often open up channels for communicating about something they may never have noticed needed exploring.

The final observation I wish to consider about the nature of the more easily resolved phobias is that the story they contain includes information about sexuality and/or attachment experiences that the person is both drawn to and unable to assimilate. In the parental response I fabricated, the references to the tiger address indirectly issues of loss of control, biting, penetration, and body damage—the stuff of sexual fantasies gone awry—and punishment, abandonment, sibling rivalry—attachment relations gone awry. Fantasies and pathogenic beliefs about castration, primal scene, impregnation, phallic females, penis envy, and the like, and/or about abandonment, coldness, antagonism, death, and the like are presented as the information gleaned by the analysts in this issue. Since some analysts, usually those using object relational and self psychological theories, emphasize attachment conflicts, and others, usually classists, emphasize sexual conflicts, we can ask: does it matter? If we assume equal sensitivity to the patient, can we say that language is a vehicle for organizing information of such a plastic nature that words such as *penetrating, dominating, cutting off, privacy, exciting,* and the like bridge sexuality and attachment. Sexuality and attachment relationships address major conundrums that baffle easy understanding such as: where do babies come from, why death, and why do mother and father treat me, or each other, the way they do. These are novelties that fascinate and overload the groping child and adult. It is noteworthy that other puzzles (where do the stars come from) and dangers (hunger, economic ruin) are rarely if ever the stuff from which phobias are made.

I should like now to consider the more troubling phobias, those which are central to the illness. The treatment of these phobias is often lengthy and the outcome more variable. Examples are the patient with the phobia to sounds reported by Meyer and Maletic, the syphilophobia patient reported by Meissner, and the cancer phobic patients, one reported by Moraitis, and one mentioned by me, who had successful resolutions after long, difficult analyses. Rocah's patient's airplane phobia and panic attacks in closed rooms had a less satisfactory outcome, and several contributors note that the treatment of many phobia patients, especially those with agoraphobias, have had disappointing outcomes. Spira, in tracing Freud's changing views, concludes that one class of agoraphobias may correspond to Freud's formulation of an actual neurosis, that is one of biological origins, while another class fits the formulation of compromise formation from intrapsychic conflict. Moraitis describes these patients as behaving like patients in a post-traumatic state who need comfort and reassurance. They are controlling and demanding, with tendencies to make the analytic treatment a ritualistic process devoid of uncertainties and novelty. Rocah notes the extraordinary vehemence of her patient's demand, the rigidity of her perceptions, her spitefulness when the analyst made an error, and the aggressiveness and tenacity of her suffering. Repeated sequences of negativistic panic, storms following each piece of understanding led the analyst to shift her focus to how the patient processed information.

How do these protracted, often refractive, phobic illnesses differ from the discrete more easily analyzed phobic symptoms? I suggested that in creating a more circumscribed phobia the person resolved a state of dialectic tension by pulling together contents and feelings into an encoded story. The patient could not uncode the information condensed into the story, but sought assistance from others to offer both safety and decoding. The basic tension between fear and security was relieved by the unresolved overload of novel information being safely rendered unknowable in the phobic story, the phobia object or situation becoming the designated source of danger while security lay in avoidance (activating the aversive system) and in seeking the help of the wise guide who can make exploring the novel feel safe. The severe phobic illnesses often demonstrate problems in all three areas. First the information contained in the phobia does not remain circumscribed. The phobic story acts like a magnet pulling in more and more associated conflictual difficulties. This is what makes the case of Little Hans so fascinating—the phobia moves from phallic rivalry issues, to issues about procreation, to issues about defecation, with varied persons involved centrally in each. Using Gedo's hierarchy, the story may start out as a Mode IV issue but will gather in elements from earlier (or later) modes. It is not sufficient for analysand and patient to construct one or two model scenes (Lichtenberg, 1989; Lachmann & Lichtenberg, in press) to understand and resolve the enigma of the phobia, but must continue to unearth a lode of unconscious information that seems at times boundless.

Second, patients vary greatly in their openness to or reluctance to explore the novelty of uncoding information about themselves. This is Moraitis's singularly important clinical finding in distinguishing between the two phobic groups he identifies. I suggest that resistance to exploring novelty can originate not only from fear of the unfamiliar but also from a deeply felt affiliative loyalty to pathologic belief systems (Weiss & Sampson, 1986) derived from family mores. I believe clinging to familiar distortions may have been a factor in Gedo's and Rocah's cases and in phobic states of children of holocaust victims.

Third, not all analysts can possibly possess the skill and experience needed to achieve the delicate balance between decoder and reassuring guide intuitively supportive of the timing of reprogramming desensitization to fear. If the phobic configuration expands so that each gain is followed by a widening range of conflicted information becoming incorporated, and if the patient displays relatively strong resistance to the need to confront ever-changing novel revelations, the burden on the analyst to manage to be both a source of safety and decoding intensifies. In a number of the cases reported, the analyses were long and difficult, but the analyst succeeded despite the difficulties. Rocah's experience, which I do not believe is unusual, documents a failure. My view of her case and others like it is that the focus of the analysis of necessity shifts. The analyst can no longer focus on decoding the multiple stories of the phobias and helping the patient to understand his or her aversive responses to the revelations. The focus becomes centered on the failures of the analyst to convey a reliable source of safety. While the analyst's agenda may be to interpret the meaning of the phobia, the patient's agenda has now shifted to complaints about the analyst's empathic failures and to demands on the analyst to provide selfobject experiences—especially the restoration of an idealizing transference. Past experiences of failed dependence, of fear induction rather than reduction, and deficient regulation of humiliation, guilt, and other aversive affects are drawn into the transference, making the establishment and restoration of a stable idealizing experience more difficult. Rocah's patient exemplified this desire for the security-providing reader of the unconscious message in her demand for an unimpeachable authority worth listening to and a magic wand. She claimed sadly that the analyst's actions convinced her that no human intervention could live up to her expectations and undo the effects of the past. The analyst had failed the test of shaman or exorcist, although she certainly appeared to have made a valiant effort.

Panic

Fear, anger, and startle are innate responses that serve as signals calling for awareness, first by caregivers and later by the self, of the need for remedial action to deal with an aversive stimulus. The responder to the signal, first parent, then parent and self, then self alone if need be, must recognize the source of the aversive stimulus and plan a suitable response—cognition being central to the desirable effect. Panic, rather than a signal, is an alarm. Panic triggers action. Cognition is momentarily shunted out of the system. The individual has to fight against and overcome the innate program of alarm to reinstitute thought and planning. An example of the effect of panic occurred to me in my junior year of medical school. I had witnessed one home delivery with a senior and was then sent out to do my own. As the productive labor reached a climax I did a pelvic examination, and, when it dawned on me that what I felt was a buttocks not a head, I panicked. I struggled desperately to remember what I had read about breech deliveries. Something about three names and a maneuver. I tried to use my photographic memory to read the page, but it was blank. All the while, amidst the shouts of the woman, my hands were active—doing something, in fact, successfully performing the maneuver and delivering a healthy baby, after which I collapsed in a chair to recover.

The understanding of panic as an alarm paralyzing cognition and triggering action is the basis for the extensive training of programmed action-patterns for soldiers, pilots, surgeons, and athletes, who are expected to encounter panic and need to rely on automatic response patterns. Panic occurs under many circumstances. The prototypic example of rapid rising alarm is an obstruction in breathing—the symbolic equivalent of drowning used by Gedo's patient. Rapid disturbances in equilibrium and forced restraint of movement are other physical alarm triggers. Other disturbances of physiological regulation (hunger, thirst, constipation, diarrhea, sleep loss) have slower rises of fear turning to panic. Panic may also occur in each of the other motivational systems: threats to sexual functioning, to cognitive loss in school examinations, and other triggers to shame and embarrassment, to the loss of availability of one's central figures of attachment, and to antagonism and rage rising to uncontrollable proportions.

New studies denote additional sources. First, many children have a neurophysiological vulnerability to panic, some showing a strong genetic familiar factor. Second, many infants reveal an aversive response of withdrawal and shyness when confronted with any unfamiliar stimuli. Kagan et al. (1987) reported on 60 children who, at 21 and 30 months, were shy, cautious, and inhibited. In response to unfamiliarity and challenge they demonstrated brain and autonomic nervous system responses that led the Kagan group to postulate that they had a different threshold of responsivity to uncertainty in limbic and hypothalamic structures. A subgroup of 13 within the inhibited group had a high and stable heart rate in response to novelty. As I indicated with respect to this subgroup, "When a fundamental response pattern is supported by physiological patterns that activate rapidly and consistently as present in 13 of the inhibited children, the possibility of ameliorative efforts being successful diminishes" (Lichtenberg, 1989, p. 280). Third, while we picture shy children clinging to their mother's leg and hiding behind her skirts, detailed infant observation reveals that many of these infants evidence aversive withdraw from the stimulus of their own mother's attachment overtures. Ainsworth (1979) and Sroufe (1979) found that at one year of age 20 to 25 percent of children observed in departure-reunion experiments were avoidantly attached to their mothers. They characteristically ignored her leavings and returns, often diverting their attention and becoming hyperaware of some object in the playroom. When observed at home, these young toddlers became demonstrably fearful at signs of the mother's departure. The mothers of these infants were observed to be angry with their children and insensitive to their signals. They were generally unresponsive emotionally and unable to establish physical contact without being jarring, unpredictable, or overstimulating.

These findings indicate that infants and/or parents who are hyperreactive to stimuli outside of a narrow spectrum establish interactions which Busch and his colleagues aptly call fearful dependency. These infants then perceive slight variation as a panic-threatening novelty and their parent, who either can't protect them or actually will expose them, as unreliable, provocative, and a source of humiliation rather than comfort and safety. Thus one factor leading to panic disorders is a neurophysiological vulnerability, especially when present in several family members.

Another factor leading to panic disorders is the repetitive

exposure to fear induction. Children subjected to episodes of physical abuse and the constant threat of it have a hair-trigger response elevating fear to panic. Unfortunately, experiences of this sort leave memories that press on the adult and promote repetitions when they are parents. Fear and anger, panicky avoidance, and antagonistic abusiveness (Meissner) are thus entwined in varying proportions, with defensive efforts interspersed.

A further factor is the major traumatic episode that leads to shock, temporary psychic paralysis, and an after state of disruptive sense of self. Car and airplane accidents, panic experiences in fires, head injuries, war, and holocaust experiences all create situations which when reexperienced in dream or associations may trigger a panic attack.

Whatever its source, an affect state of panic becomes itself a source of an intense fear of repetition, so that panic may occur as a fear of panic. For some patients a combination of the physiological concomitants of panic—increased heart and breathing rate or a bodily sensation associated with a fatal condition—may act as a signal misidentified as a sign of physical doom. This typical hypochondriacal syndrome differs from phobias in that it does not have a condensed encoded story, and from other panic episodes for which neither trigger nor affective symptom is associated with internal bodily danger. Panic episodes can also be followed by a great reluctance to be anywhere but in one's own home among familiar people and resources, such as the phone. The fear is of having a panic, not of being in the agora (market) with its symbolic meanings. These fears of panic and the restrictions they bring about are, I believe, different from the agoraphobias and other phobias that occur after diffuse tensions rather than after panic episodes. They do not necessarily involve a condensed story of specific symbolic meanings, but more closely approximate a negative conditioning experience. All three types of disturbances: hypochondriacal panic states, phobias, and generalized panic states may be present, each requiring separate understanding. Sometimes in the long, difficult phobic illnesses the phobia fails to elicit from the decoder successful responses of help to face novelty. If panic ensues, the clinical picture shifts from one in which interpretation of symbolic representation is possible to one that requires containment of alarm states that trigger action at times of cognitive paralysis.

Panic disorders are unlike phobias in the essential feature of shunting cognition out of the sequence of alarm followed by action. Unlike phobias, where analysis can feel on solid familiar ground in pursuing a basically exploratory approach with some desensitizing where needed, panic disorders "may benefit most often from a treatment that combines neurophysiological, cognitive-behavioral, and psychodynamic approaches" (Busch et al.).

REFERENCES

Beebe, B. & Stern, D. (1977). Engagement, disengagement and early object experiences. In *Communicative Structures and Psychic Structures,* ed. M. Freedman & S. Grand. New York: Plenum, pp. 35–55.

Brenner, C. (1975). Affects and psychic contents. *Psychoanal. Q.,* 44:5–28.

_____ (1976). *Psychoanalytic Technique and Psychic Conflict.* New York: Int. Univ. Press.

Demos, V. (1985). The elusive infant. *Psychoanal. Inquiry,* 5:553–568.

Emde, R. (1983). The prerepresentational self and its affective core. *Psychoanal. Study Child,* 38:165–192.

Fraiberg, S. (1982). Pathological defenses in infancy. *Psychoanal. Q.,* 51:612–635.

Freud, S. (1909). Analysis of a phobia in a five-year-old boy. *S.E.,* 10.

Gaensbauer, T. (1982). Regulation of emotional expression in infants from two contrasting caretaker environments. *J. Amer. Acad. Child Psychiat.,* 21:163–171.

Kagan, S., Reznick, J., & Snidman, M. (1987). The physiology and psychology of behavioral inhibition in children. *Child Development,* 58:1459–1473.

Lachmann, F. & Lichtenberg, J. D. (in press). Model scenes: Implications for psychoanalytic treatment. *J. Amer. Psychoanal. Assn.*

Lichtenberg, J. (1989). *Psychoanalysis and Motivation.* Hillsdale, NJ: The Analytic Press.

Renik, O., Spielman, P., & Afterman, J. (1978). Bamboo phobia in an eighteen-month-old boy. *J. Amer. Psychoanal. Assn.,* 26:255–282.

Sroufe, L. A. (1979). The coherence of individual development: Early care, attachment, and subsequent developmental issues. *Amer. Psycholog.,* 34:834–841.

Stern, D. (1985). *The Interpersonal World of the Infant.* New York: Basic Books.

Weiss, J. & Sampson, H. (1986). *The Psychoanalytic Process.* New York: Guilford.

1616 Eighteenth Street, N.W.,
Washington, D.C. 20009

Epilogue

THE IN-DEPTH EXPLORATION of any psychological phenomenon, no matter how well circumscribed clinically, will inevitably necessitate the broadening of the boundaries of the exploration in order to place it in context. Phobias are no exception.

For a long time the clinical and theoretical study of the phobic symptom was dominated by the imaginative interpretation of the patient's unconscious fantasies and their vicissitudes. It is hard to overestimate the enormous appeal of such interpretations for the analyst. It can be compared to the reaction Freud reported when he visited the Acropolis, "So all this really does exist, just as we learned in school."

With time, however, the analyst's excitement has been tempered by the fact that many of the phobic patients neither share the analyst's excitement about the interpretations of the unconscious fantasies nor improve clinically as a result of such interventions.

The preceding contributions illustrate that the contemporary psychoanalyst has taken notice of the fact that all phobias cannot be effectively dealt with simply by the interpretation of their symbolic meaning. Instead, our contributors, to various extents, approach phobias as a manifestation of a more general and basic pathology, structurally and developmentally.

This development has important clinical implications because the phobic symptom is no longer the main focus of the analyst's attention, but a stepping stone in addressing the deeper level of psychopathology upon which the whole personality organization rests.

In order to meet this challenge, the psychoanalyst, when analyzing phobias, must be careful not to be seduced by the characters and plot of the patient's fantasies and those of his own. Instead, the analyst needs to develop a broader concept of the psychoanalytic process that takes into account contemporary advances from within and without the field of psychoanalysis as they pertain to phobias.

George Moraitis, M.D.
Issue Editor

www.ingramcontent.com/pod-product-compliance
Ingram Content Group UK Ltd.
Pitfield, Milton Keynes, MK11 3LW, UK
UKHW022201190926
475702UK00003B/139
9780881639506